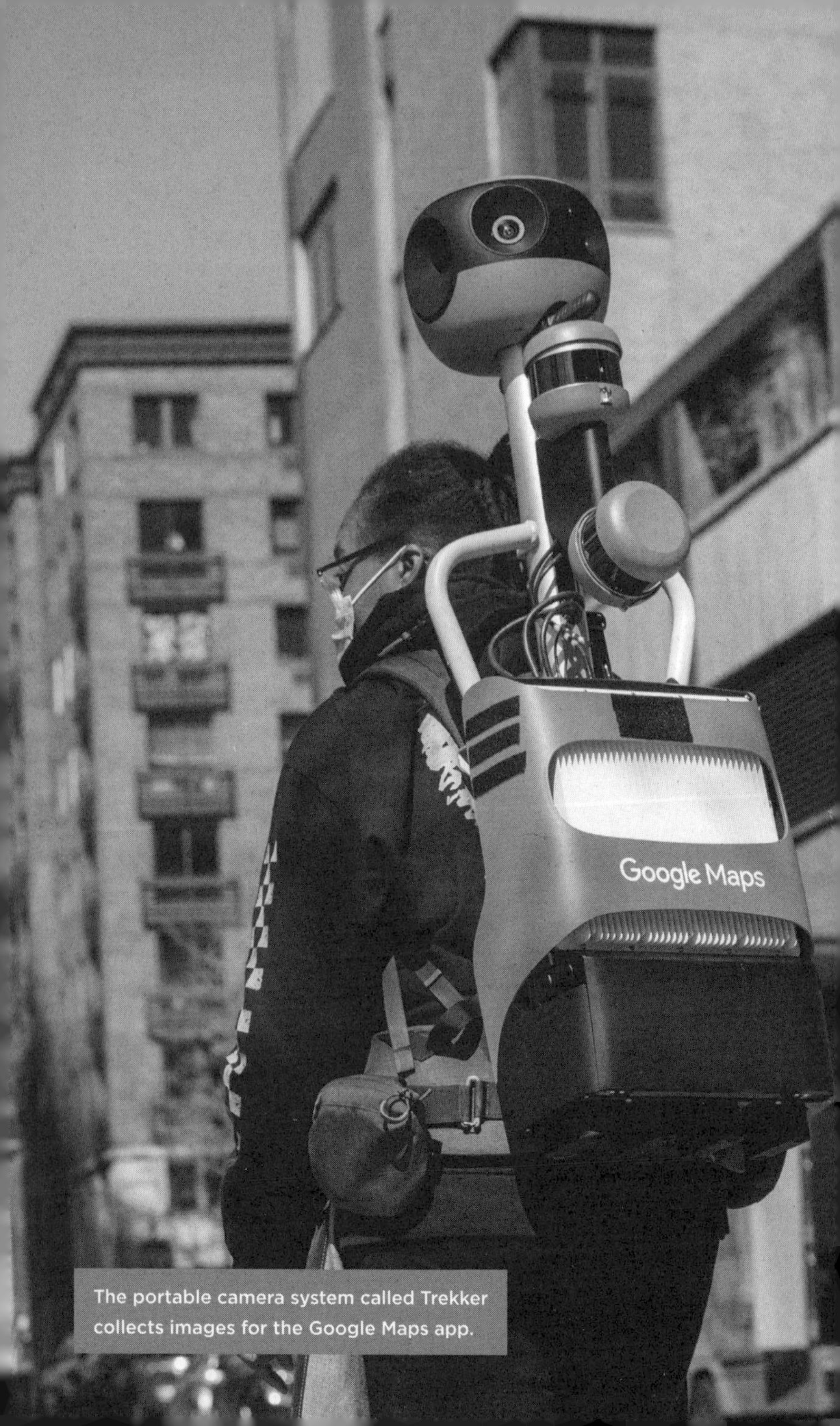

The portable camera system called Trekker collects images for the Google Maps app.

GOOGLE

CREATIVE COMPANIES

NELL MUSOLF AND SARA GILBERT

JAICO PUBLISHING HOUSE

Ahmedabad Bangalore Chennai
Delhi Hyderabad Kolkata Mumbai

Published by Jaico Publishing House
A-2 Jash Chambers, 7-A Sir Phirozshah Mehta Road
Fort, Mumbai - 400 001
jaicopub@jaicobooks.com
www.jaicobooks.com

Published in arrangement with
The Creative Company
2140 Howard Drive West,
North Mankato, MN 56003, USA

To be sold only in India, Bangladesh, Bhutan,
Pakistan, Nepal, Sri Lanka and the Maldives.

Design by Graham Morgan
Art direction by Tom Morgan
Edited by Jill Kalz

Images by Alamy (Alex Segre, Bob Elam), Getty (Chris Hondros, Des Jenson/Bloomberg, Getty Images / Handout, Justin Sullivan, Kim Kulish, MARTIN BUREAU, Ramin Talaie, Steve Proehl, Ulrich Baumgarten), Pexels (Anna Shvets, Firmbee.com, Mati Mango, Pixabay), Unsplash (Brett Jordan, Madhur Chadha, Pawel Czerwinski, Stephen Phillips - Hostreviews.co.uk, Suzy Brooks), Wikimedia Commons (Alvandria, Andrew Henkelman, Nguyen Hung Vu, TechCrunch, Till Niermann)

GOOGLE
ISBN 978-93-49358-55-3

First Jaico Impression: 2025

Printed by
Parksons Graphics Pvt. Ltd., Mumbai

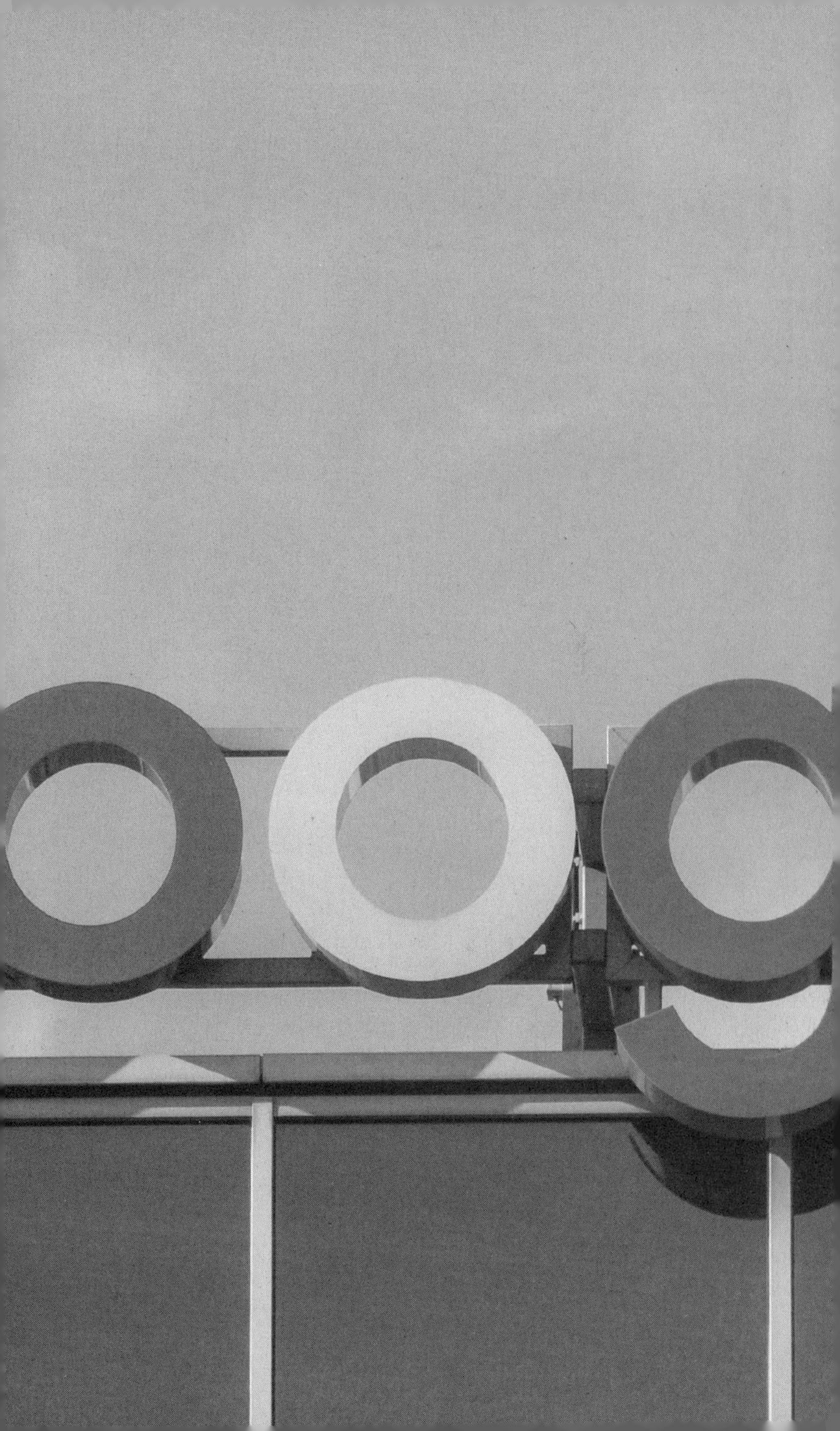

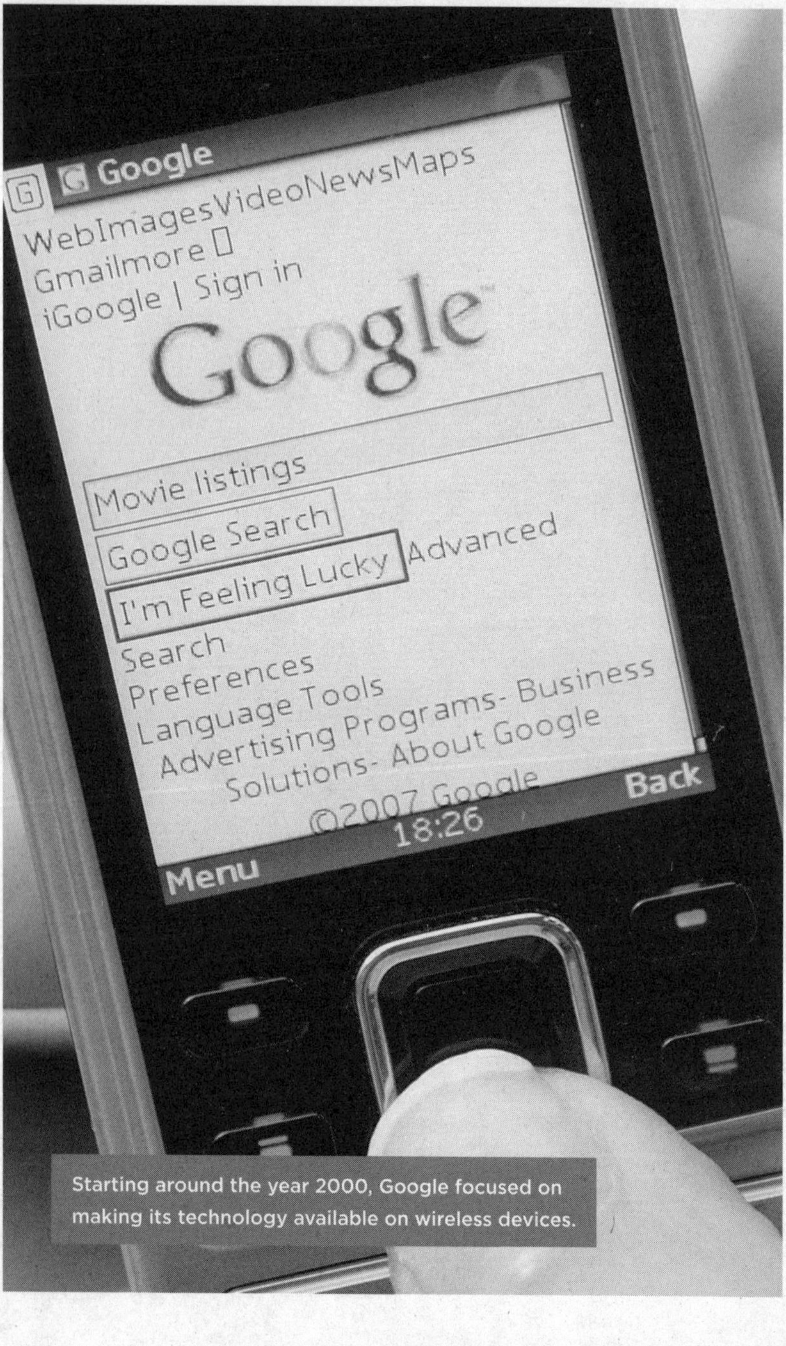

Starting around the year 2000, Google focused on making its technology available on wireless devices.

CONTENTS

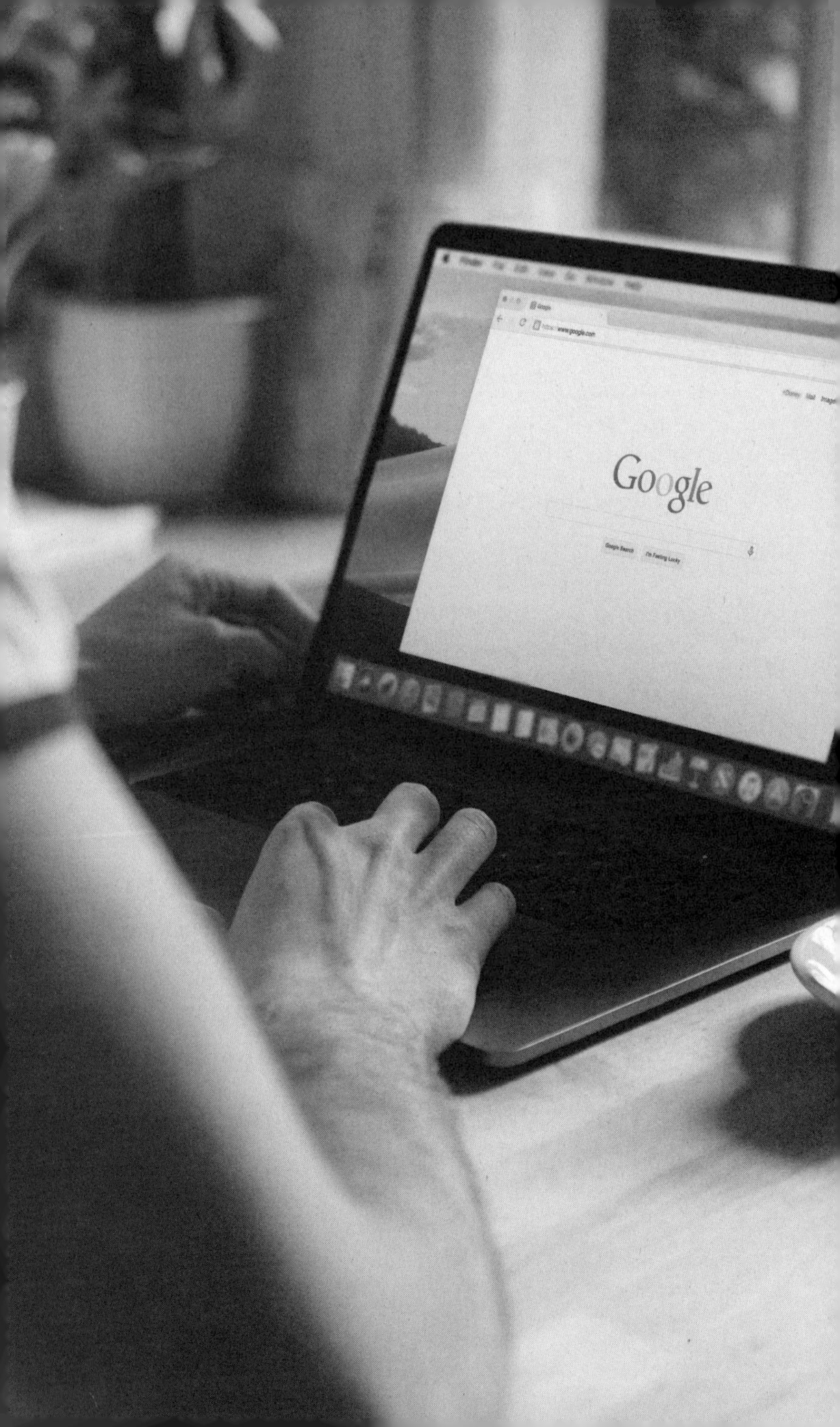
Google

Introduction

On September 7, 1998, the **search engine** company Google officially became Google Incorporated. Founded by Larry Page and his business partner, Sergey Brin, while graduate students at Stanford University, Google was a joint vision the pair made a reality.

OPPOSITE: Each day, about 8.5 billion searches are done worldwide with the Google search engine.

It wasn't until Page and Brin were given an investment of $100,000 by Andy Bechtolsheim in 1998 that Google really took off. With Bechtolsheim's seed money, Page and Brin were able to rent office space for their company—a garage in Menlo Park, California. The humble surroundings didn't bother the young **entrepreneurs**, though. All they needed was a place where they could work around the clock.

Page and Brin believed in Google from the start. Even so, it's doubtful they envisioned a future where Google would be the number one search engine in the world. And they couldn't have predicted the phrase "Google it!" would become synonymous with "Look it up!"

What started in Larry Page's California dorm room became a worldwide success story in a remarkably short amount of time. It's a success story that keeps on growing.

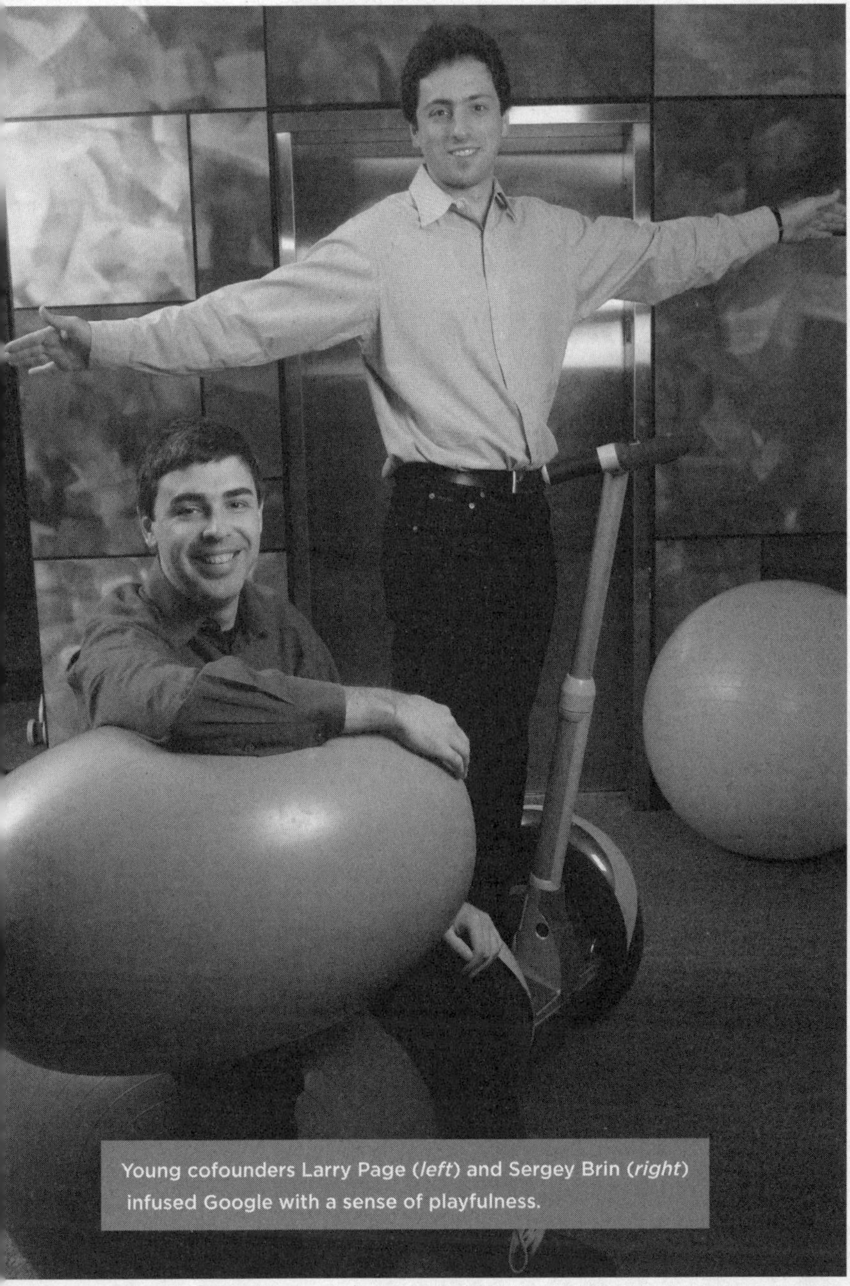

Young cofounders Larry Page (*left*) and Sergey Brin (*right*) infused Google with a sense of playfulness.

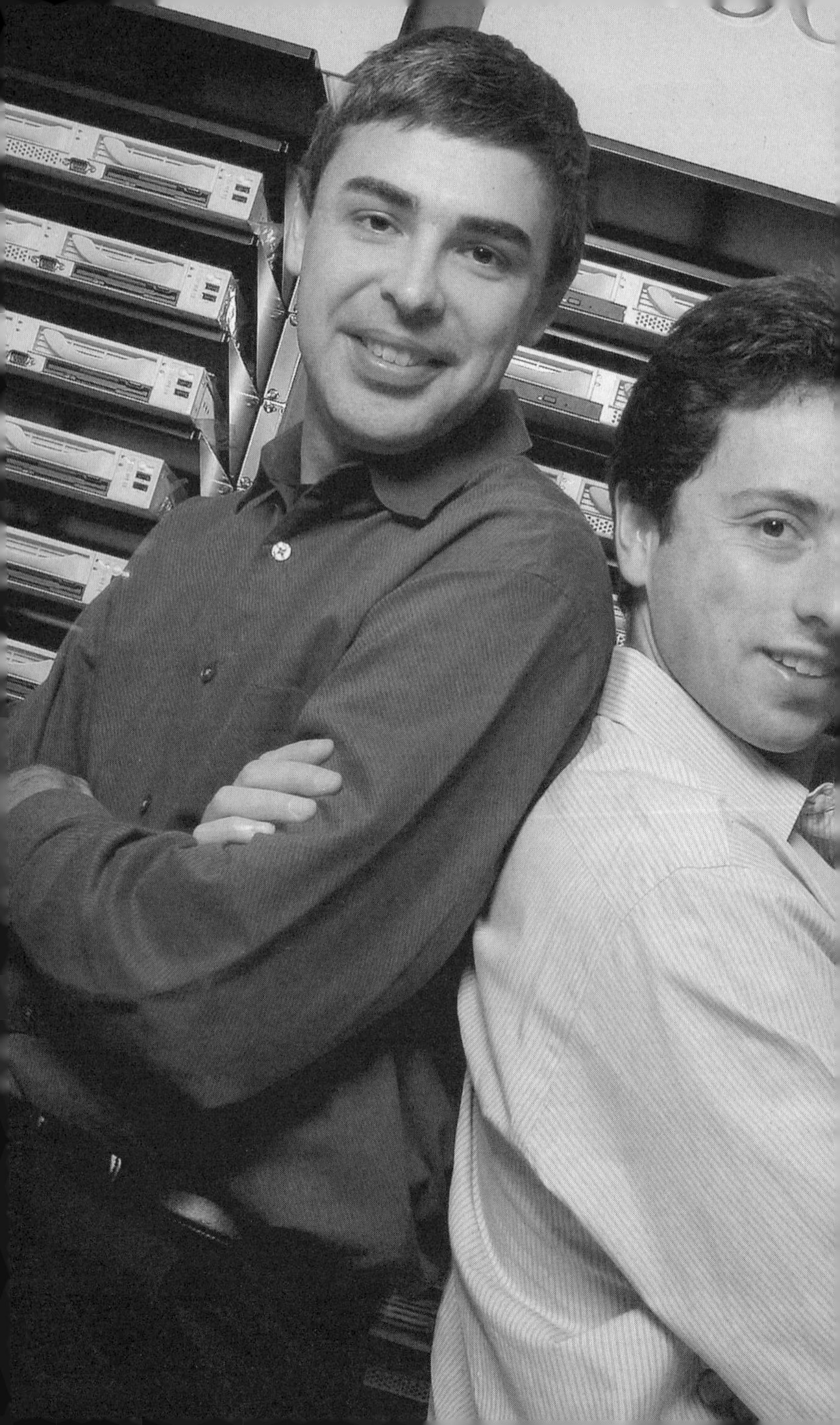

Hello, Google

Larry Page was in Palo Alto, California, in the spring of 1995 when he met Sergey Brin. Page was visiting the campus of Stanford University, which had just accepted him into its prestigious PhD program in computer science. The two men—both bright, curious, and up for a good-natured argument—hit it off.

OPPOSITE: Larry Page (*left*) and Sergey Brin (*right*) pose inside the data storage room of Google's headquarters in 2003.

That friendship blossomed when Page returned to Stanford the following fall. Almost as soon as the new friends and the rest of the students and faculty moved into the brand-new William Gates Computer Science building, they began working together on a possible **doctoral thesis**. They wanted to build a product to download the entire World Wide Web and figure out a way to search it using links. Page had decided that the number of links pointing to a particular site was an indicator of that site's popularity and relevance. He called his system of ranking pages through links "PageRank," a play on his own name.

By early 1997, PageRank had paved the way for a search engine called BackRub, a name that was soon replaced by the name Google. For the logo, Page and Brin opted for a plain white background with "Google" spelled out in bright primary colors. The design was a contrast to other search engines of the time that usually featured home pages filled with ads, colors, and confusion. "If you went to a design firm and asked for a home page for a search engine, you would never get that," said Stanford professor Dennis Allison. "It doesn't have any animation or metallic colors, and there is no sound or lights. It flies completely in the face of the common belief that people love to find their way through the noise."

Allison was one of many in the Stanford community who caught on to the

Google phenomenon in 1997, when the search engine was made available to students, faculty, and administrators. Now that Page and Brin had users accessing their growing database, they needed more **hardware** to store all the information they were searching for. But as graduate students, they had no budget for new **hard drives**. So, they bought inexpensive parts, built their own machines, and hung around the loading docks on campus, looking for unclaimed computers that they could "borrow." They even maxed out their credit cards buying an exceptionally large amount of storage on disks. When they ran out of space in the office they shared with other graduate students, they turned Page's dorm room into a data center.

The two young men couldn't continue running their search engine on a shoestring budget. The ideal

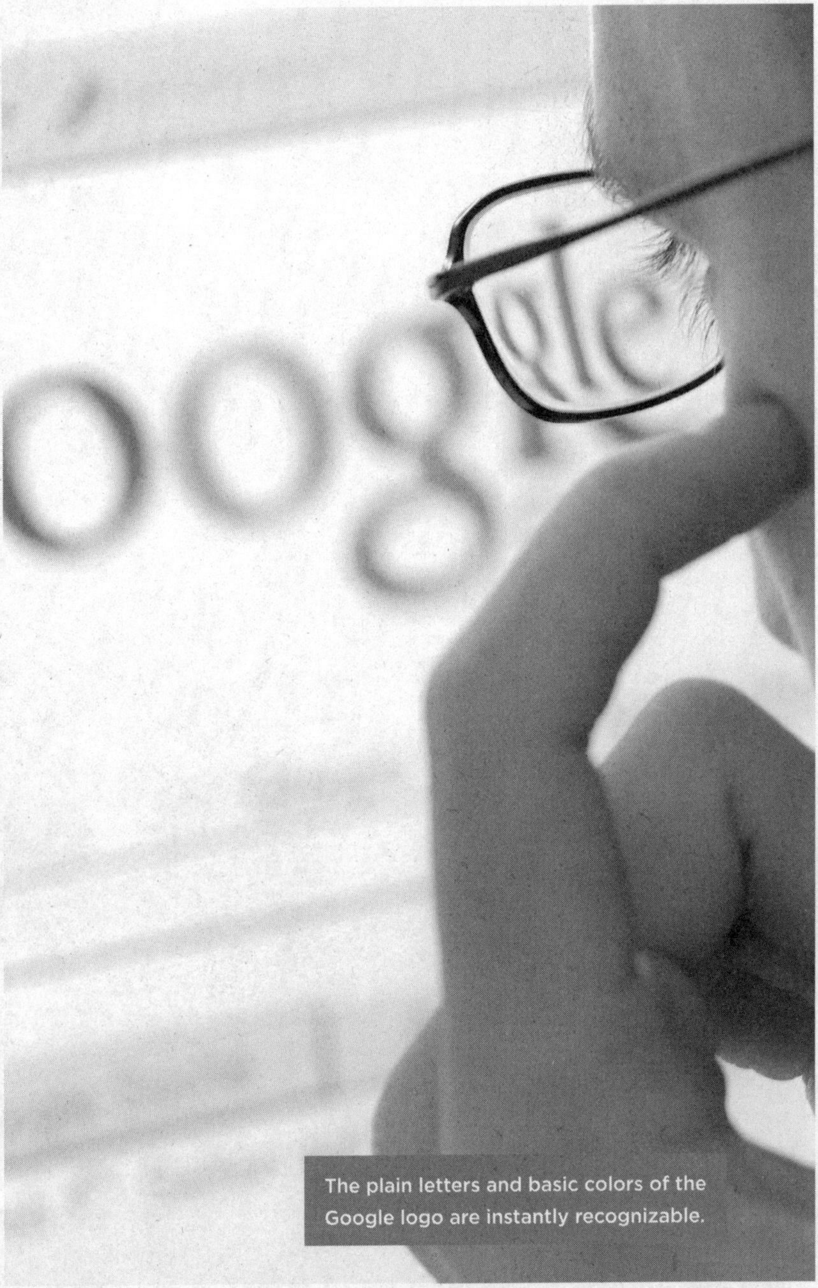

The plain letters and basic colors of the Google logo are instantly recognizable.

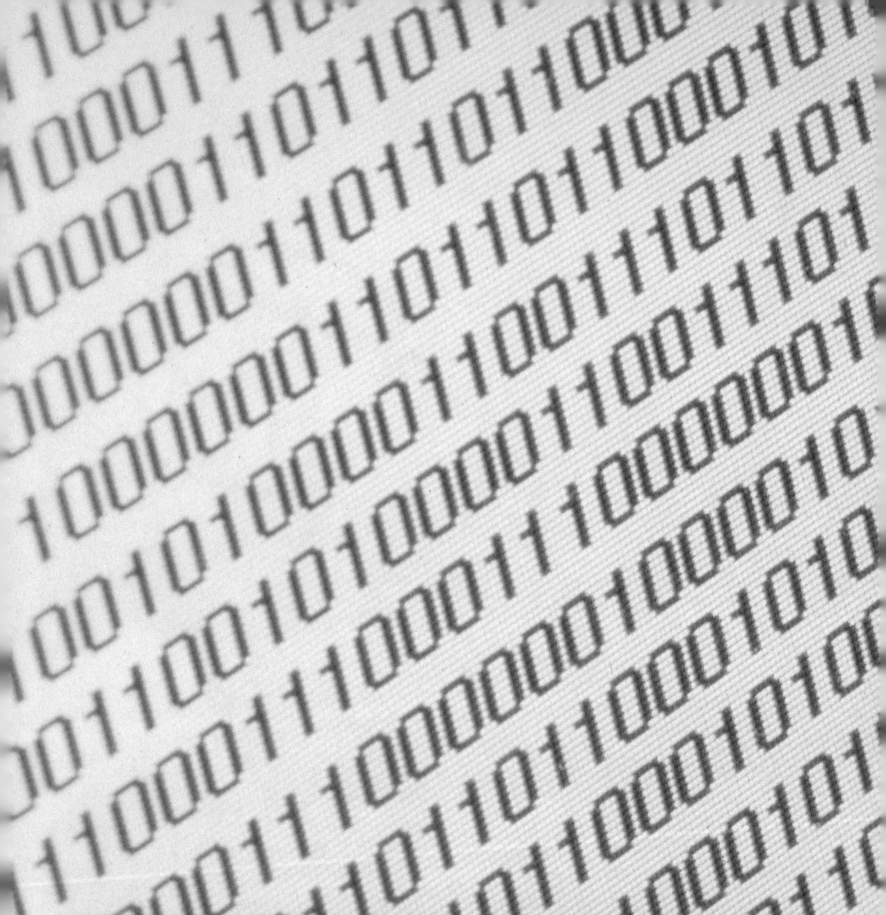

A Name of Numbers

Google's name is the result of an innocent misspelling. While still at Stanford, a fellow graduate student suggested the name "Googleplex"—which is spelled "googolplex." It is 10 raised to the power googol—which represents the number 1 followed by 100 zeros. Larry Page suggested shortening it to Google. A quick check revealed that it was still available as a domain name, so he and Sergey Brin registered the name and scrawled it on a whiteboard in the office: google.com. The next morning, another office mate left a note for them: "You misspelled it. It is supposed to be G-o-o-g-o-l."

solution, they decided, was to license their search technology to an existing company. It was 1998, and the frenzy of emerging technology companies made for several potential partners. But all the contacts they made with Internet companies such as AltaVista, Excite, and Yahoo! turned into dead ends. Most companies seemed more interested in making money on advertising than in improving their search engines.

The lack of outside enthusiasm for their product made Page and Brin more determined to improve it. They sent letters to families and friends, encouraging them to use the search engine and asking for suggestions on ways to improve it. They asked everyone they knew to spread the word about the site. And they constantly tweaked the way Google looked and worked. They added short summaries for each search result so that users could immediately see which results were most relevant to them.

As their database grew, one of Page and Brin's professors introduced them to Andy Bechtolsheim, cofounder of Sun Microsystems and vice president of Cisco Systems. Page and Brin impressed Bechtolsheim with what they were doing. They explained how they thought Google could make money by licensing their search technology to other Internet companies or even selling their ideas to a large company. "This is the single best idea I have heard in years," Bechtolsheim said. "I want to be a part of this."

Bechtolsheim wrote a check to Google for $100,000. There was a slight hitch, however. At that time, the company didn't officially exist! After the meeting, Page had to tuck that check into his desk drawer until he and Brin **incorporated** the company and opened a bank account. That happened on September 7, 1998. To celebrate the moment, the two men went out to breakfast at Burger King.

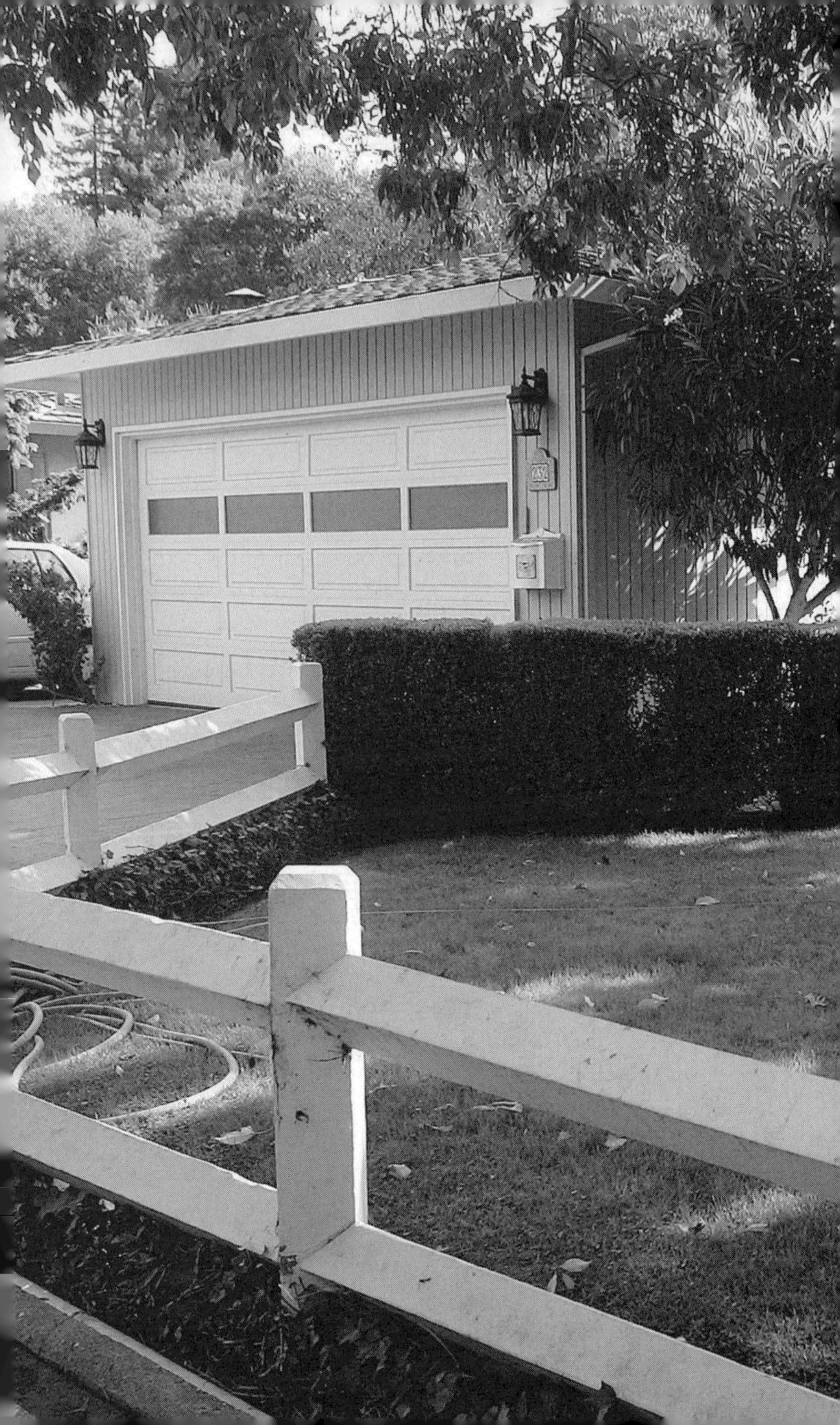

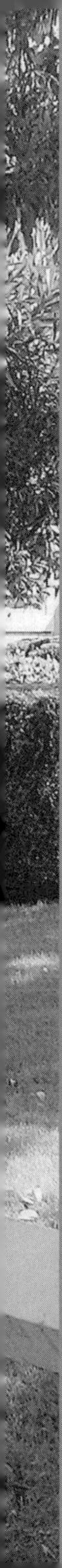

The Little Engine That Could

The first official Google office was in a garage in Menlo Park, California. Page and Brin had opted to leave Stanford in 1998 without their PhDs to focus on their new business. They rented from a friend, Susan Wojcicki, for $1,700 a month. Although they didn't know it at the time, Wojcicki would again play an important role at Google in the future.

OPPOSITE: Google's first headquarters was a modest rented garage space at 232 Santa Margarita Ave., Menlo Park, California.

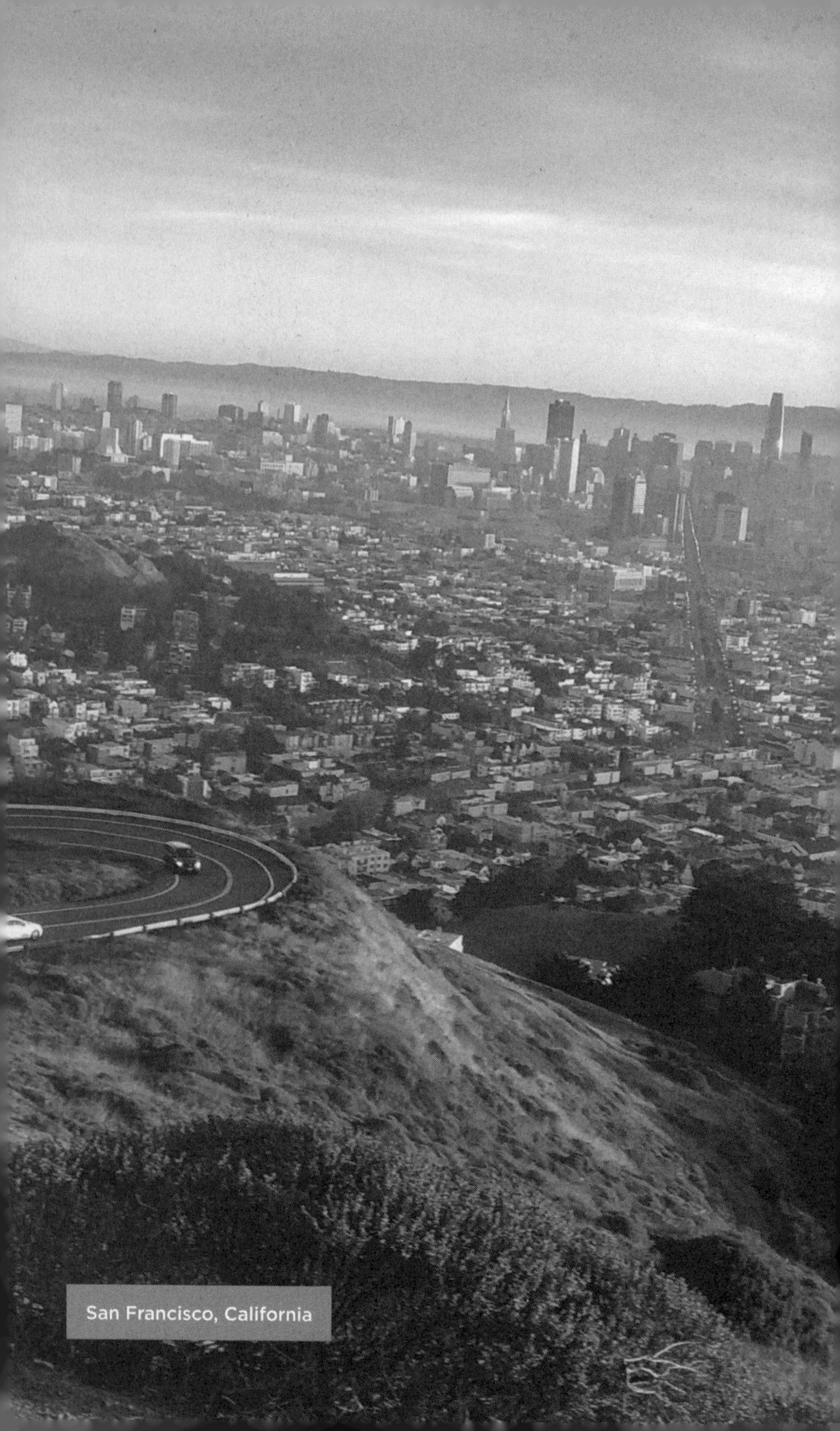

San Francisco, California

It didn't take long for the company to outgrow the garage. After five months, Google and its eight employees moved to a new office in downtown Palo Alto. By then, Google has been mentioned in magazine articles and newspaper features. It was named a "Top 100 Web Site and Search Engine for 1998" by *PC Magazine.* It had even secured a client: Red Hat, a software firm that licensed search technology. But despite the attention, Google was running out of money. Money was vital for the expansion of its search technology and the company's capabilities.

Page and Brin decided to seek out **venture capital** for funding. They looked to Silicon Valley, an area near San Francisco where many high-tech companies are based. After researching their options, they approached two of the most established firms

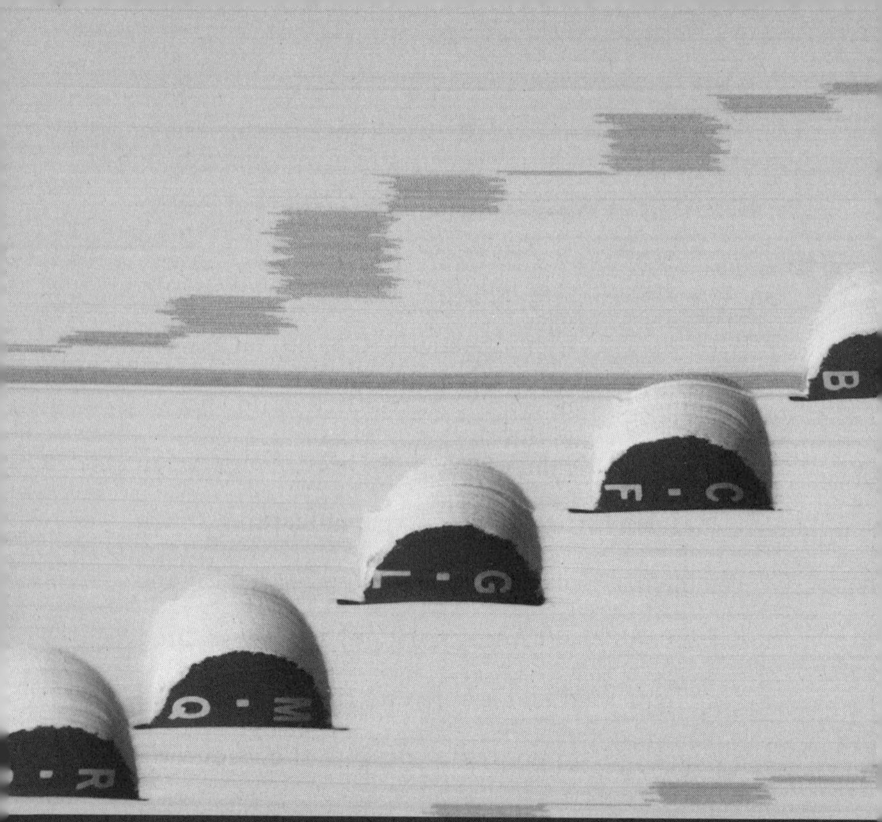

The Verbing of Google

Google's founders never considered their company's name anything more than a noun meaning a very large number, representing the enormous size of their indexes. But users of the search engine quickly turned the name into a verb. In 2006, *Merriam-Webster* defined the word *google* as a **transitive verb** meaning "to use the Google search engine to obtain information about (a person) on the World Wide Web." Thomas Pitoniak, the associate editor and composition manager for *Merriam-Webster*, said, "Google is a unique case. Because they have achieved so much prominence in the world of search, people have been using the word *google* as a generic verb now."

there, hoping to secure financing from both. The young men impressed the firms not only with their technology and their long-term plans but also with their enthusiasm and friendly personalities.

By the spring of 1999, both Kleiner Perkins Caufield & Byers and Sequoia Capital were ready to invest a total of $25 million in Google. But neither firm wanted to share the investment. Page and Brin were concerned that if they accepted funds from just one investor, they would lose control over their company. Although it was risky, they told both firms that the deal was off if they couldn't work together.

Neither firm wanted to lose out on what looked like a promising investment. So, they made it work. Each company would invest $12.5 million in Google, and each would have a seat on the company's **board of directors**. Page and Brin would maintain majority control. The only condition was that the young businessmen had to hire a seasoned **executive** to run the business side of things. Page and Brin saw the value of that, and they agreed.

The influx of cash allowed Google's founders to aggressively recruit top people to their company. They had already put out feelers to their friends in the industry. New employees would get **stock options** and free snacks and drinks at work.

They also had the satisfaction of knowing that millions of people were using and appreciating the software they were developing. And they would get paid well.

As 1999 ended, Google was averaging a remarkable seven million searches per day—but Page and Brin still hadn't found a way to convert those searches into a revenue stream. Although selling

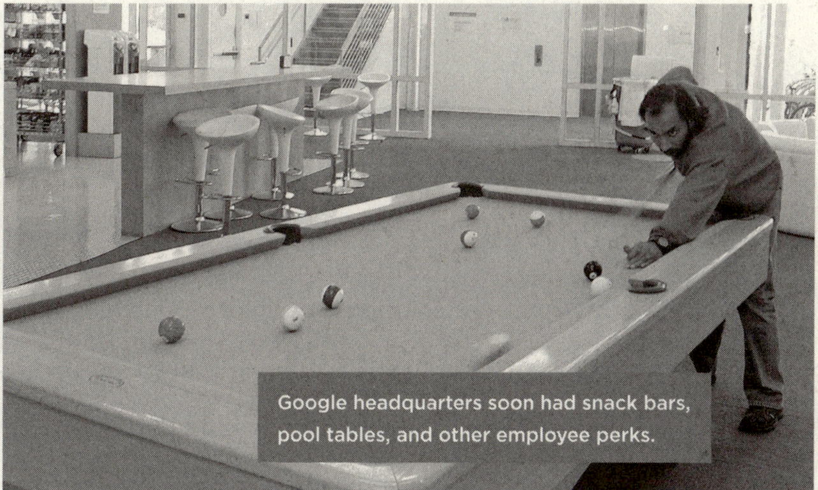

Google headquarters soon had snack bars, pool tables, and other employee perks.

ads was the obvious choice, they worried that allowing advertising on their site would conflict with the motto they had established for their company. They had hoped to differentiate it from other companies driven purely by **profits**. Search results, they believed, should always be free and unaffected by advertising. But they also were beginning to see the value of selling targeted ads that could accompany search results.

The solution they agreed upon was to sell Sponsored Links, a column of text-only links that ran on the right-hand side of the results page. The ads, like the search results, were displayed based on relevance. A formula balanced how much an advertiser was willing to pay (ads were sold in an auction format, with a "per-click" price that started at five cents a click) with how many times the ad was clicked on. The more popular ads were sent to the top of the page.

In less than three years, Google had experienced incredible growth. By the beginning of 2001, it was handling more than 100 million search queries per day—about 1,157 a second! It had set out to make those searches more convenient by establishing relationships with several wireless Internet providers, making its technology available over cell phones and other devices. By the fourth **quarter**, Google had recorded its first annual profit of $7 million.

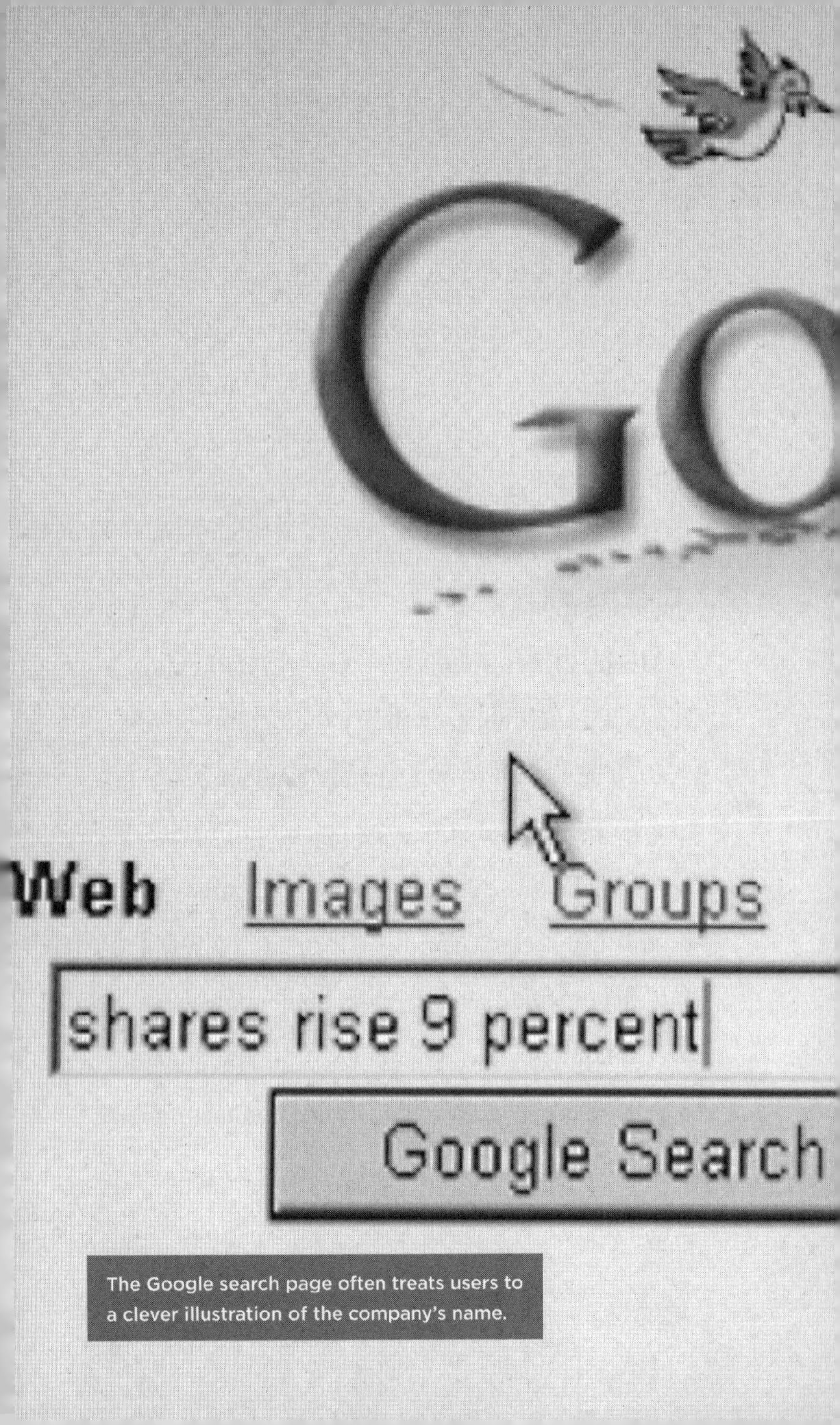

The Google search page often treats users to a clever illustration of the company's name.

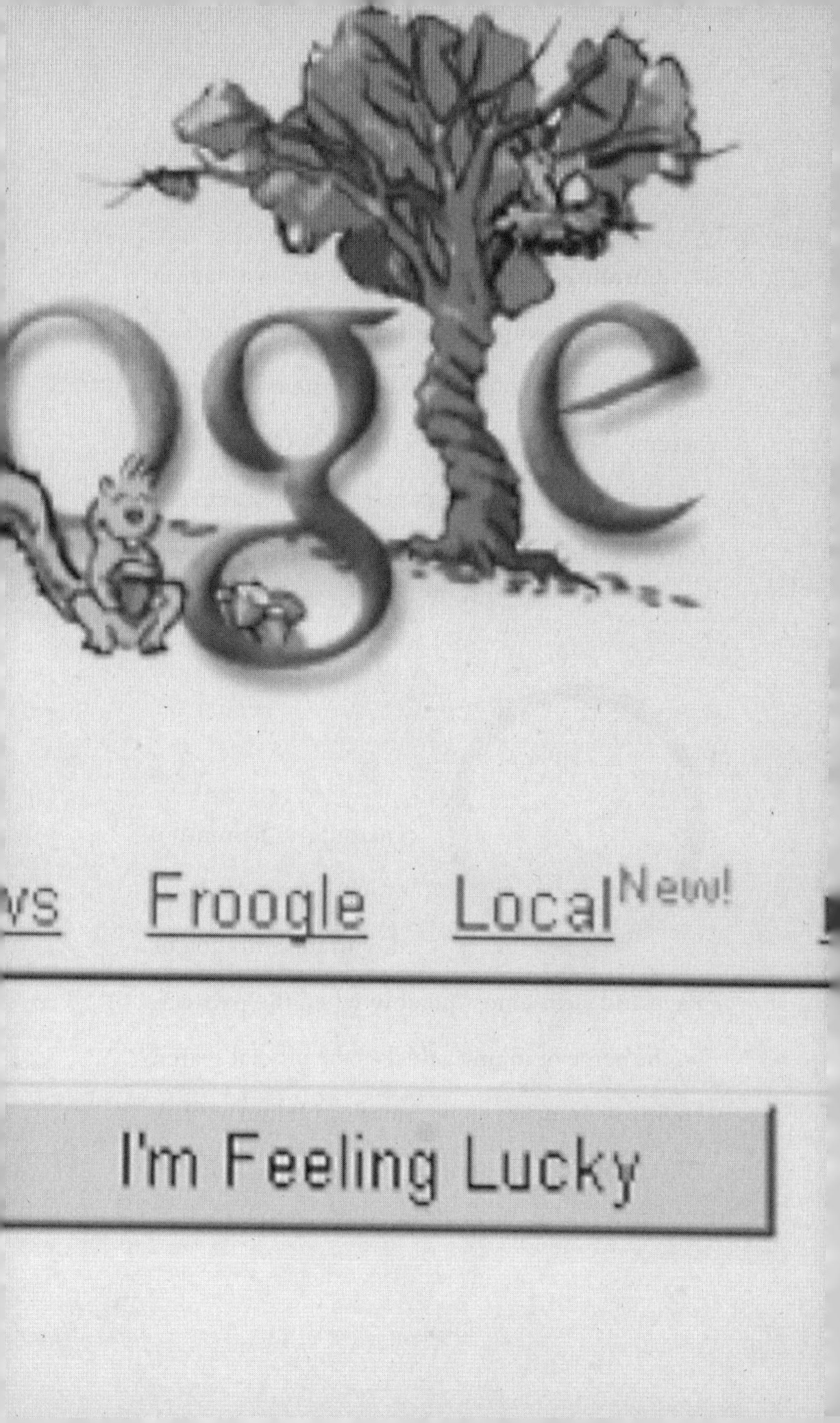
Froogle
Local New!
I'm Feeling Lucky

Guiding the company through its amazing growth spurt was Eric Schmidt, a former chief technology officer for Sun Microsystems. Schmidt became the chief executive officer (CEO) and chairman of Google in August 2001. His job was to enforce order in Google's young, creative environment.

Occasionally, Schmidt's business sense conflicted with the ambition of Page and Brin—most notably when the pair was on the verge of inking a deal as the official search engine of Internet giant America Online (AOL). AOL was asking for a huge financial guarantee from Google, as well as stock options. Although Page and Brin were willing to pay any price for the business, Schmidt wanted them to approach the deal more conservatively. The founders pulled rank on their CEO, however, and confidently completed the deal.

On May 1, 2002, AOL's 34 million subscribers found a small search box on every page that said, "Search Powered by Google." Soon, Google had also signed a deal to provide searches for the Internet provider Earthlink. More deals followed. By the end of 2002, Google's balance sheet reflected $440 million in sales and $100 million in profits. Schmidt had to admit that Page and Brin had been right to pursue those partnerships. "They were more willing to take risk than me," he said. "They turned out to be right."

Page and Brin put much of the money that was coming in back into highly creative ideas for expanding the search business—many of which came from the company's own employees. Google News, which offered free access to more than 4,500 news sources worldwide, was launched in September 2002. Froogle, a product search service, went online in test mode for the holiday shopping season a few months later. Froogle was later rebranded as Google Shopping in 2012.

Google went global by making the site searchable in hundreds of languages, from Greek and Chinese to Russian and Danish.

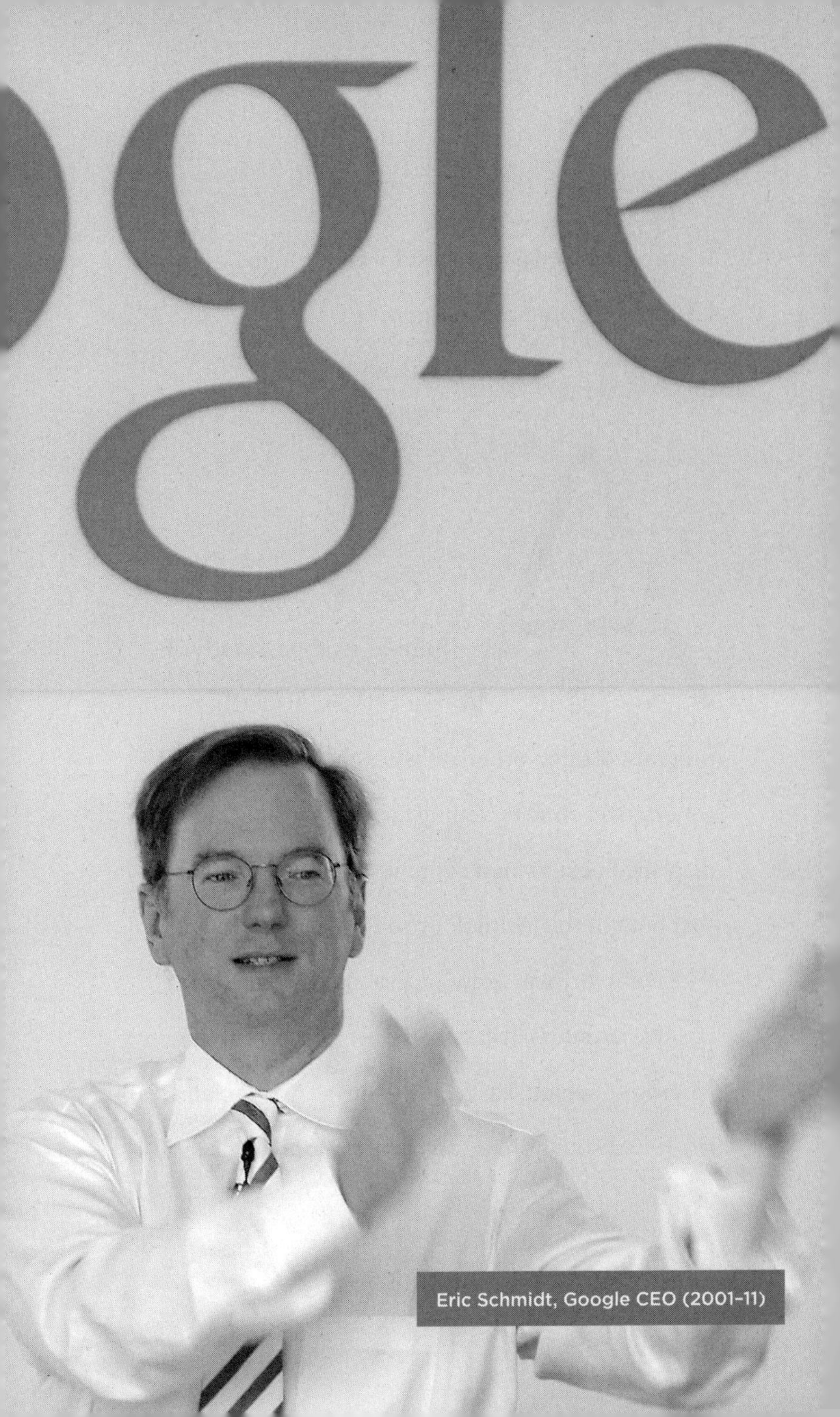

Eric Schmidt, Google CEO (2001–11)

It even included a few "just for fun" tongues—Pig Latin and Klingon, for example.

As Google's product improved, its appeal to advertisers grew. Its AdSense program offered other websites the technology to generate revenue by selling targeted ads that could be placed next to their content. Of course, each site that bought the technology sent money to Google. The company was growing fast and gaining lots of positive attention. It caught the eye of software giant Microsoft, which was reeling from a lawsuit claiming it had sought to establish a **monopoly** with its computer operating system. Google's success made Microsoft nervous about losing its top position in the software industry. Although the two companies didn't compete head-to-head, they would both try to outdo the other with new, creative ideas from that point on.

TAKEAWAY

By the beginning of 2001, [Google] was handling more than 100 million search queries per day—about 1,157 a second!

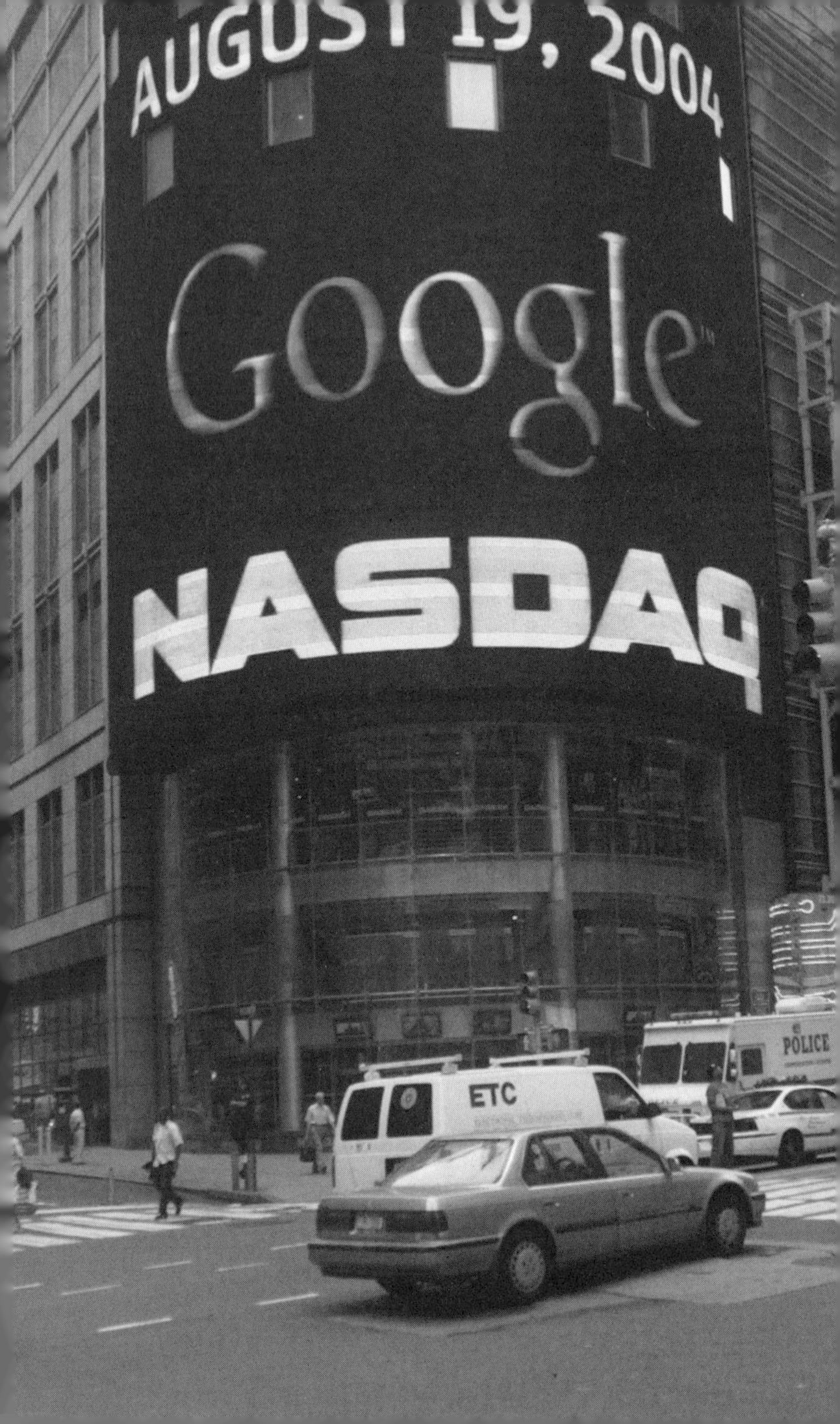
AUGUST 19, 2004
Google
NASDAQ
ETC
POLICE

Searching the Stock Market

Although business was booming in 2004, Larry Page and Sergey Brin were convinced they could do better. In particular, they knew they could do email better than such competitors as Microsoft, Yahoo!, and AOL. They wanted their version to be cheaper, easier to use, and superior in every way to the other brands.

OPPOSITE: Google opened on Wall Street on August 19, 2004, at $85 per share and closed at $100.34—an 18 percent increase in one day.

When Page and Brin announced the launch of Gmail with a press release on April 1, 2004, they expected a lot of buzz. They were, after all, offering a greater amount of online storage space—a full **gigabyte**—to all subscribers, which was still unheard of in the industry. Even better, there was no cost at all for users. But the buzz that came out of their announcement was focused almost entirely on an aspect to which they hadn't given much thought: the fact that Google intended to run targeted ads in the emails. Privacy advocates were furious that the content of emails sent and received would be scanned to find keywords that could be paired with ads. Lawmakers threatened legislation. For the first time, Google's "good boy" image had been tarnished in a very public way.

"Google is risking its reputation for honesty and

April Fools' Day

For many years, April Fools' Day was a mischievous holiday at Google. Workers were encouraged to come up with harmless pranks to share with users. One of the more successful jokes included "Google Gulp." This fictitious drink supposedly increased a user's intelligence, thus increasing the user's use of the Google search engine. "Google Book Search Scratch and Sniff" encouraged users to smell their monitors to get a whiff of a particular scent. The April Fools' Day jokes came to an end in 2020 with the advent of the COVID-19 pandemic and have not been resumed.

putting the user first with its new email service," Walt Mossberg, a technology columnist for the *Wall Street Journal,* wrote. "The problem here isn't confusion between ads and editorial content. It's that Google is scanning your private email to locate the keywords that generate the ads. This seems like an invasion of privacy."

Page and Brin were unprepared for the negative reaction to their Gmail announcement. They believed the uproar would blow over once users had a chance to experience the product. But they still consulted a lawyer. Their lawyer advised them to

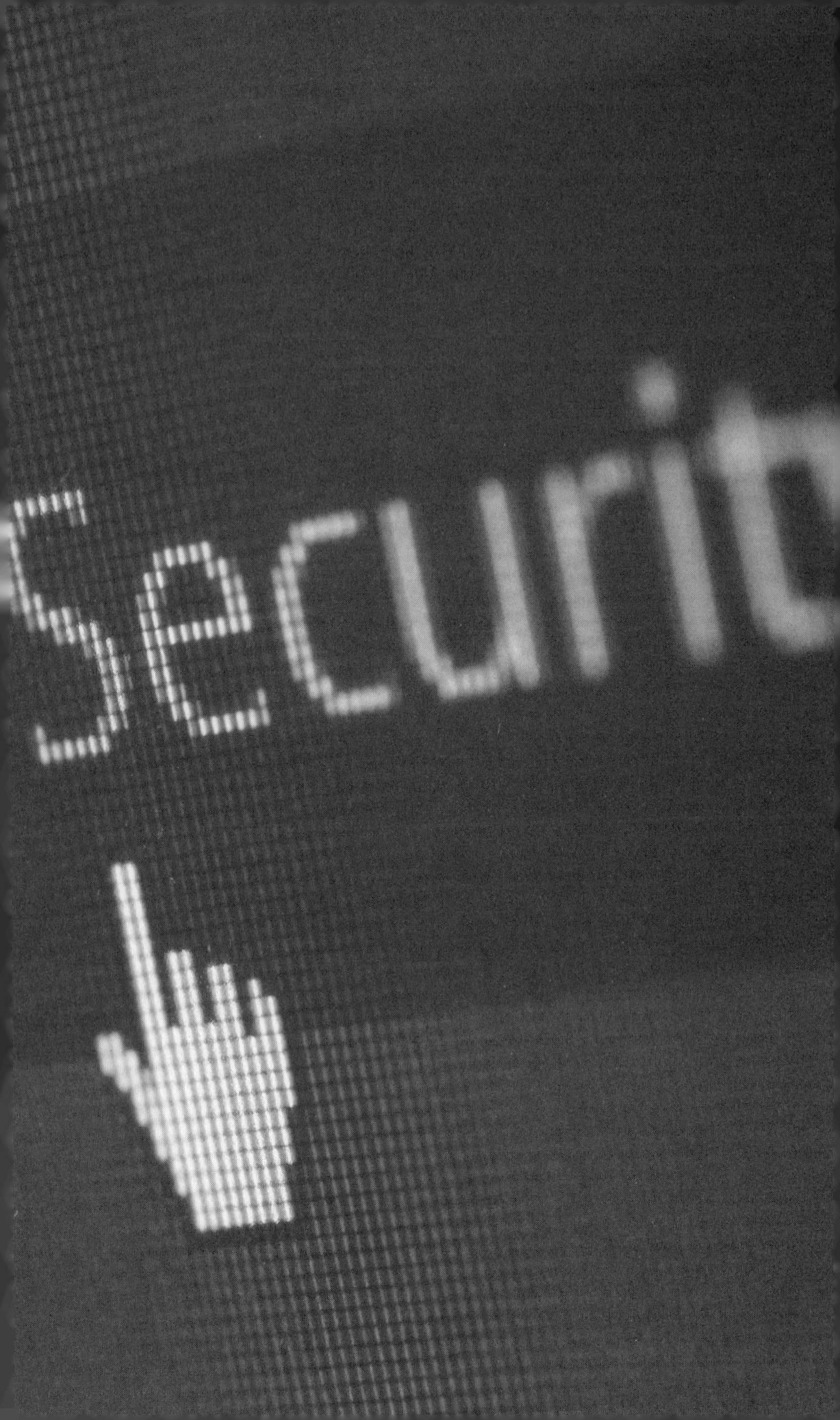
Securit

take steps to make searching email archives impossible and to strip personal information about users from their records. They did not, however, change their plans to run ads with emails.

Google's founders never anticipated privacy as an issue when they began scanning emails. They saw it as a way to improve users' email experience. They thought people would appreciate getting ads geared toward items they might be looking for.

After being contacted by numerous civil rights and privacy groups, Google made changes to how

Gmail worked. Unwanted accounts were regularly deleted, as were deleted emails. Once the privacy hiccup was handled, Gmail became hugely popular with users. In 2017, Google dropped scanning emails altogether. Gmail maintained its popularity and is currently the most used email service in the world.

The furor over Gmail was still raging when, on April 29, 2004, Google filed with the Securities and Exchange Commission (SEC) for an **initial public offering**. Although Page and Brin weren't eager to give up the freedom of private

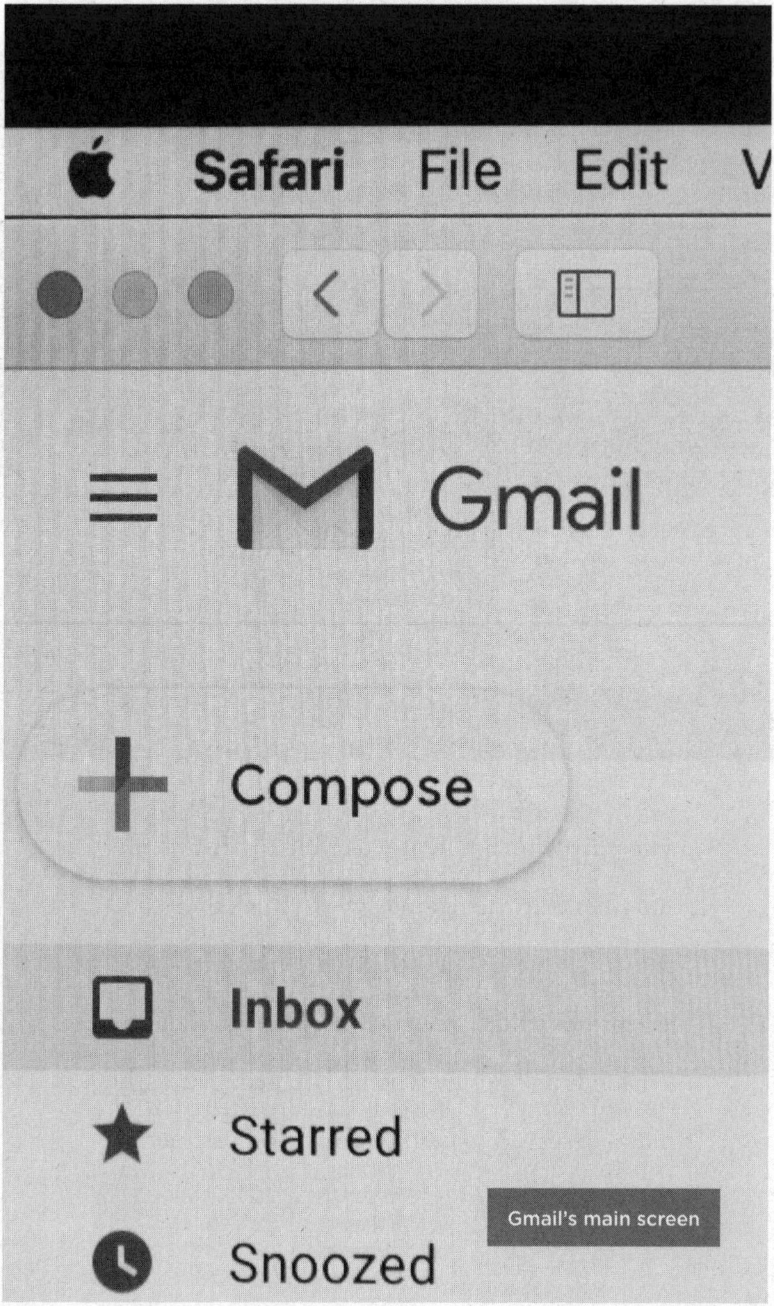

Gmail's main screen

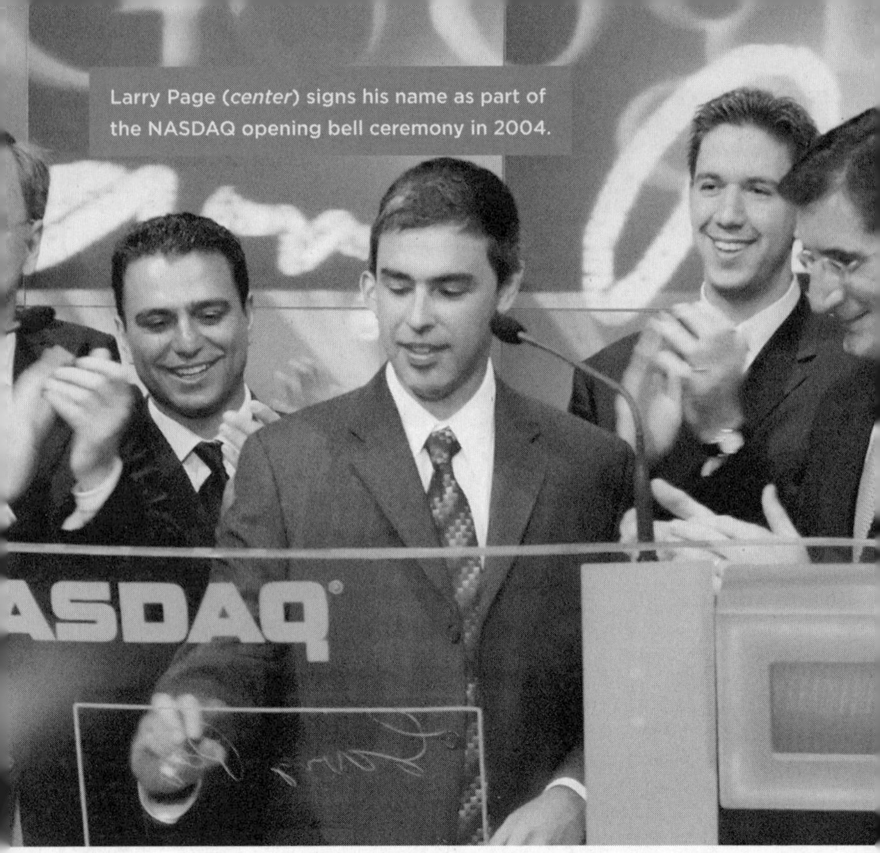

Larry Page (*center*) signs his name as part of the NASDAQ opening bell ceremony in 2004.

ownership, they knew it was time to reward the employees they had recruited with promises of stock options. They also knew that their investors—from the venture capital firms and Andy Bechtolsheim to the friends and family who had helped raise early funds—deserved to cash in on their investments.

And they knew that the infusion of cash would help their company maintain its growth and achieve new things.

On August 19, 2004, Google began trading on **NASDAQ** for $85 a share. Page went to Wall Street for the occasion. Brin stayed in California to oversee the day-to-day operations of the company. By the end of the day, both men were multimillionaires. Their company had raised $1.67 billion—among the largest totals ever raised by a technology company.

Even though they now shared Google with stockholders, Page and Brin remained in charge. They wanted to continue creating a workplace atmosphere that reflected the kind of place at which they'd like to work. The growing company moved into a huge office complex in Mountain View, California. Named Googleplex, the campus covers 68 acres (27.5 hectares) of land and has walking trails, green spaces, and access to a 5-acre (2-ha) public park located next door.

STUDIOS architecture firm designed Googleplex. They note that the **iconic** campus remains "a pivotal model for the evolution of the modern workplace for its playful approach to work as something fun and collaborative."

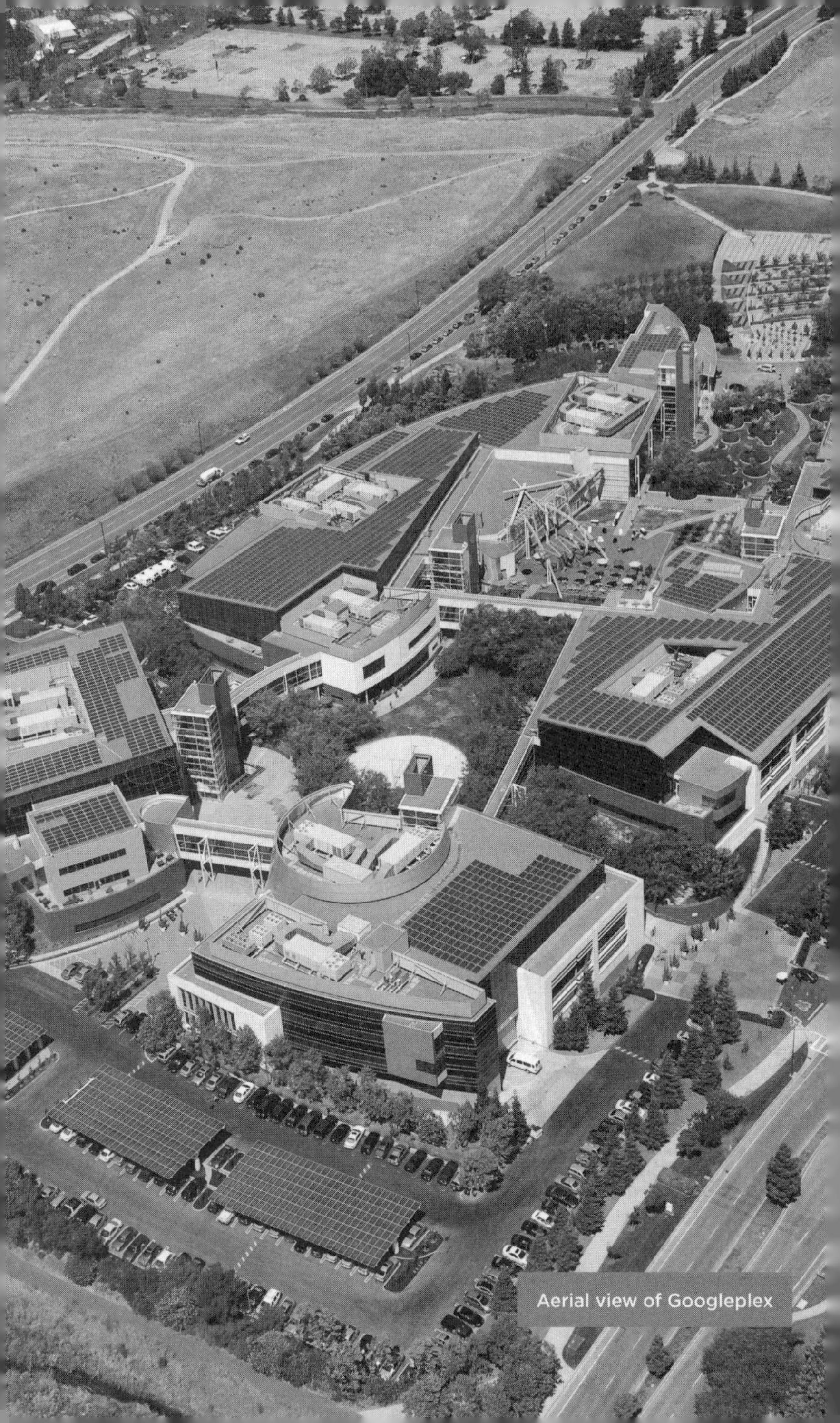

Aerial view of Googleplex

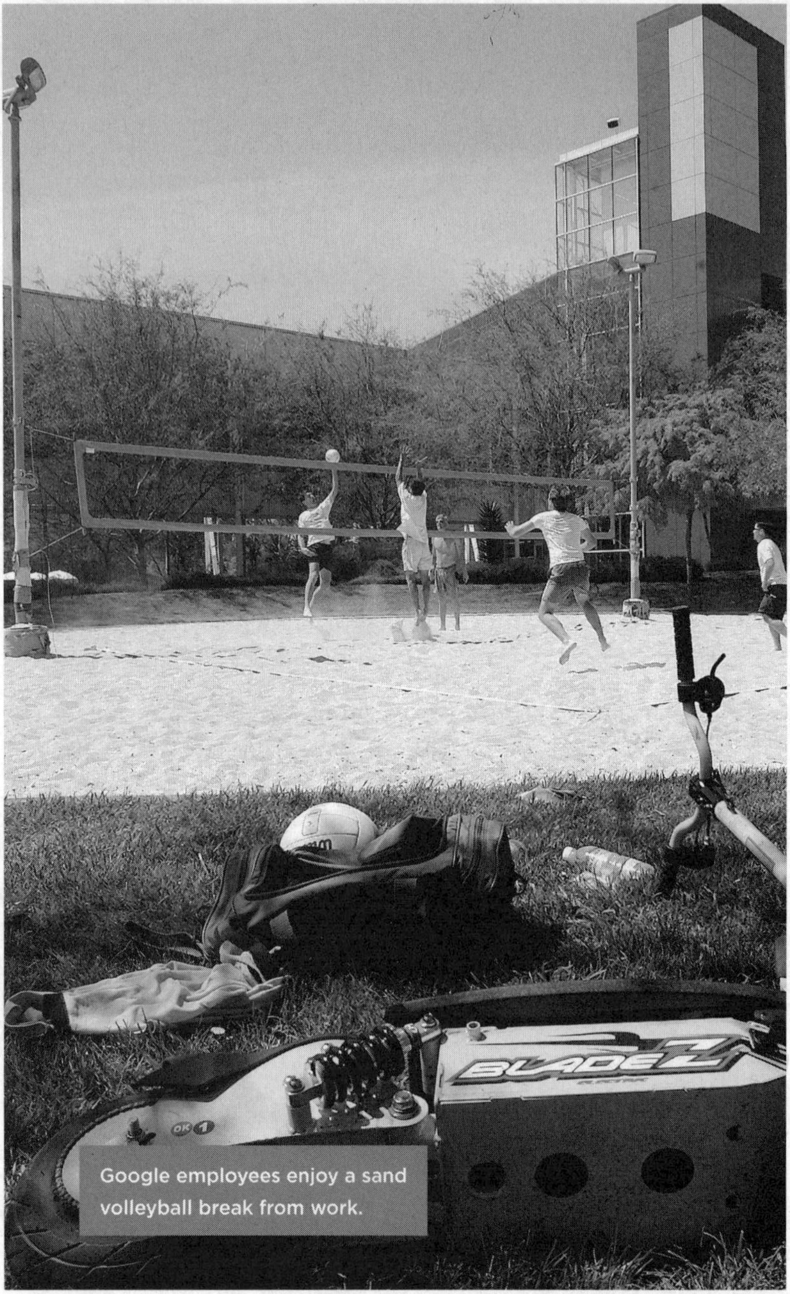

Google employees enjoy a sand volleyball break from work.

Inside the four main buildings are all kinds of amenities. Employees have access to free video games, pianos, a rock-climbing wall, a doctor's office, and laundries. There's a snack bar, a bowling alley, hair salons, and gourmet meals served three times a day. Google's management has designed an atmosphere its employees will enjoy while doing the hard work of being constantly creative.

Google employees receive lots of perks and are well paid, but there are high expectations of all workers. The leaders at Google believe that if they give employees the things that will make them happy, they will get extraordinary ideas and loyal employees in return. Employees have access to management on a regular basis and are encouraged to share opinions, problems, and any issues they might have. A culture of "belonging" has long been encouraged, with the goal that workers feel valued and respected. It's an idea that seems to be working. Google has been voted Best Place to Work multiple times since 2007.

One interesting practice at Google is what is known as "The Twenty Percent Theory." Google employees are encouraged to

TAKEAWAY

Google [leaders] believe that if they give employees the things that will make them happy, they will get extraordinary ideas and loyal employees in return.

spend 20 percent of their work week focusing on projects of their own choosing. It doesn't matter how farfetched the project might be. The Twenty Percent Theory has resulted in many successes, including Gmail.

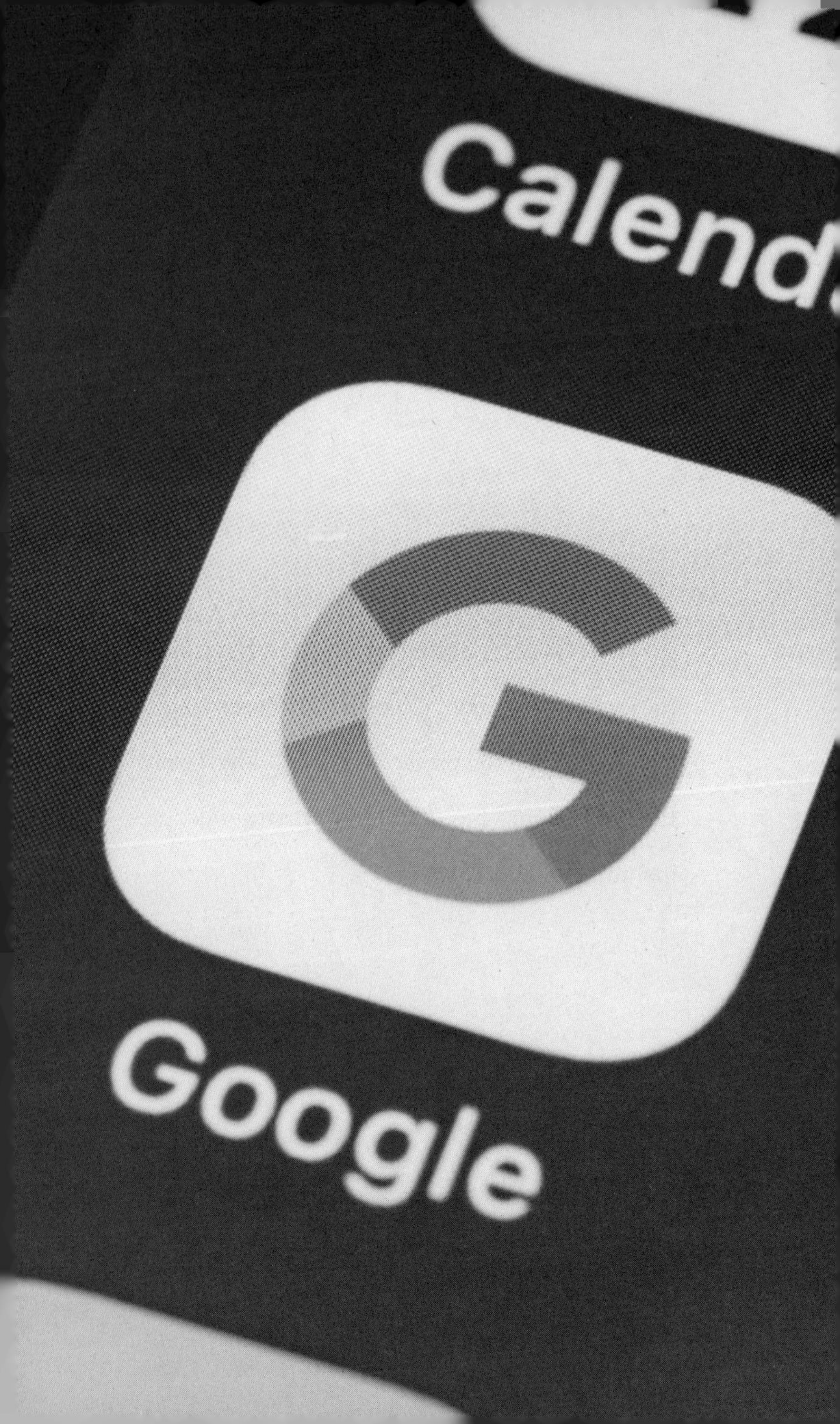
Calend
Google

Google Grows and Grows

As Google has grown, so have its applications, or apps. Google Game Store has more than three million apps for Android users to download. While some apps are more popular than others, apps are continuously being evaluated and updated by Google.

OPPOSITE: Logos for Google apps, such as Google Maps and Google Play, echo the iconic four-color "G" used for the search engine.

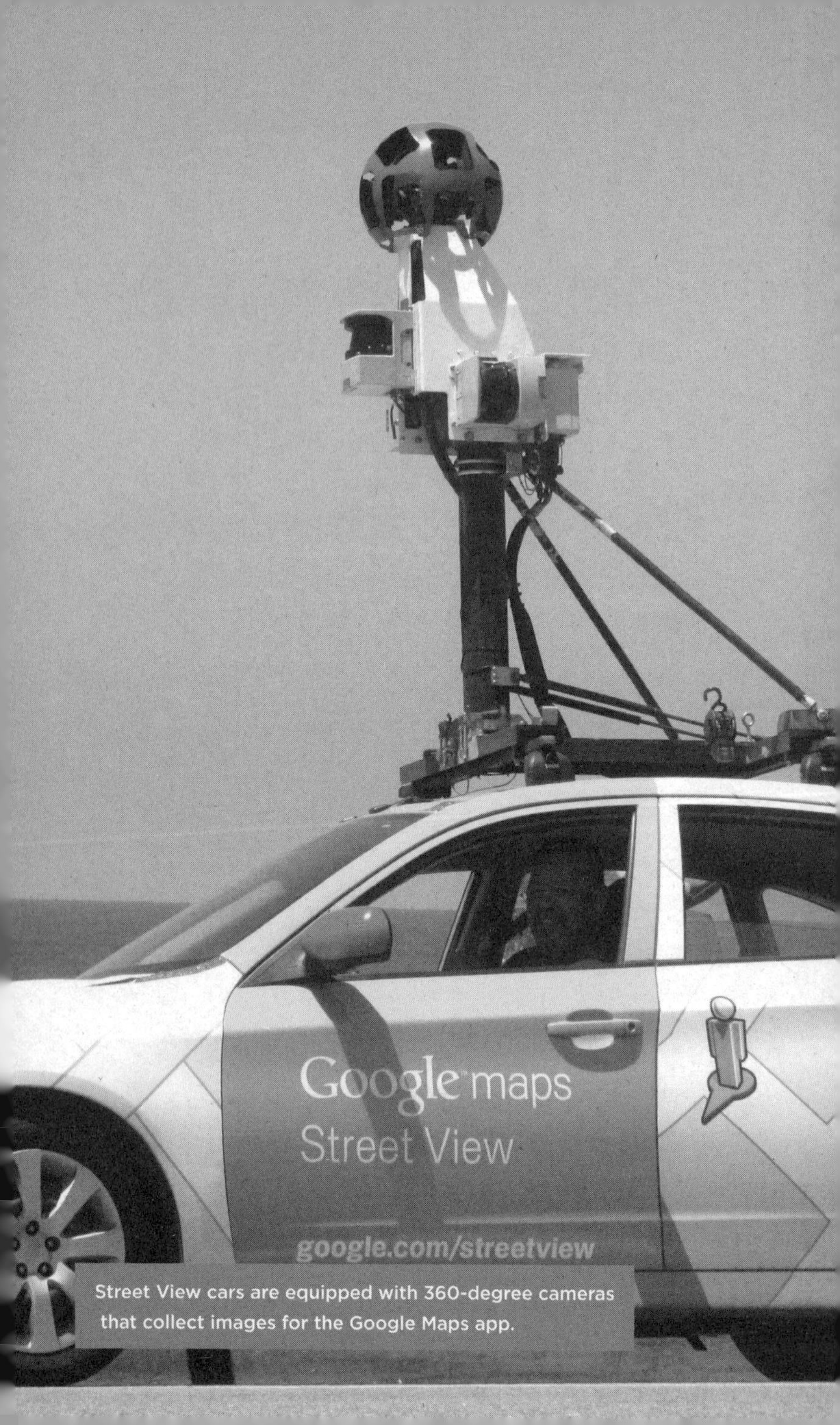

Street View cars are equipped with 360-degree cameras that collect images for the Google Maps app.

Google Chrome is a highly popular app. It is known as a **cross-platform** search browser that combines software components from other browsers. It is the default browser for Android.

Google Maps began in 2005. The app allows users to get directions, figure out distances, and keep track of where they have been. Google Maps includes Street Views, which are pictures of virtually any location a person wants to see. In 2018, wheelchair-accessible routes were added to help people with accessibility needs. Google Maps is one of the most popular apps the company has.

Google Play is also popular. It first came to light in 2012, combining Android Market, Google Music, and Google Books under one app. Users can rent and purchase movies and television shows through the app.

Google Images was developed after Google employees noticed how often people searched for pictures of celebrities and other images. The app has approximately one billion searches *per day*.

Arguably, the most famous Google app is YouTube. The streaming service began as a video-sharing site and has become one of the company's most popular success stories. YouTube was started in 2005 by three former PayPal employees: Jawed Karim, Steve Chen, and Chad Hurley. It featured uploaded videos on virtually any subject, and it was an immediate hit. The following

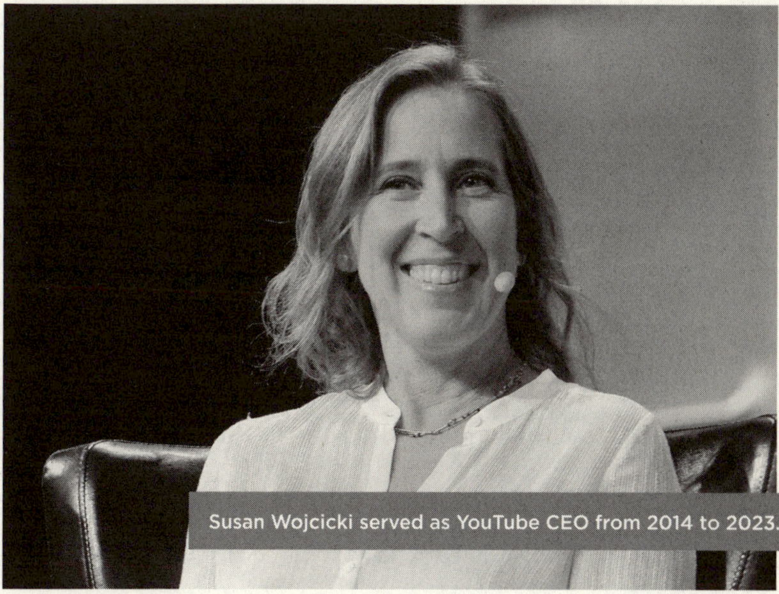

Susan Wojcicki served as YouTube CEO from 2014 to 2023.

year, Google bought YouTube for $1.65 billion. Even though Google owned it, YouTube remained a separate—and extremely successful—**entity**. Bringing a part of Google's early history full circle, the CEO of YouTube was Susan Wojcicki, Page and Brin's former landlord.

YouTube currently has more than 2.6 billion users, making it the second biggest social media site in the world, following Facebook. More than half the world's population uses YouTube, watching news, television shows, movies, how-to videos, biographies, history, and more. And if people aren't watching YouTube, they might be uploading their own videos for others to view. Almost four million videos are uploaded on an average day.

Since its inception in 1997, Google has grown by leaps and bounds and in all sorts of directions. Where can it go from here? Where does it want to go? For Page and Brin, the sky might not be the limit. It might be time to go even farther.

Alphabet was the name of a group of international companies managed by Google. While Google has always been known as a company primarily

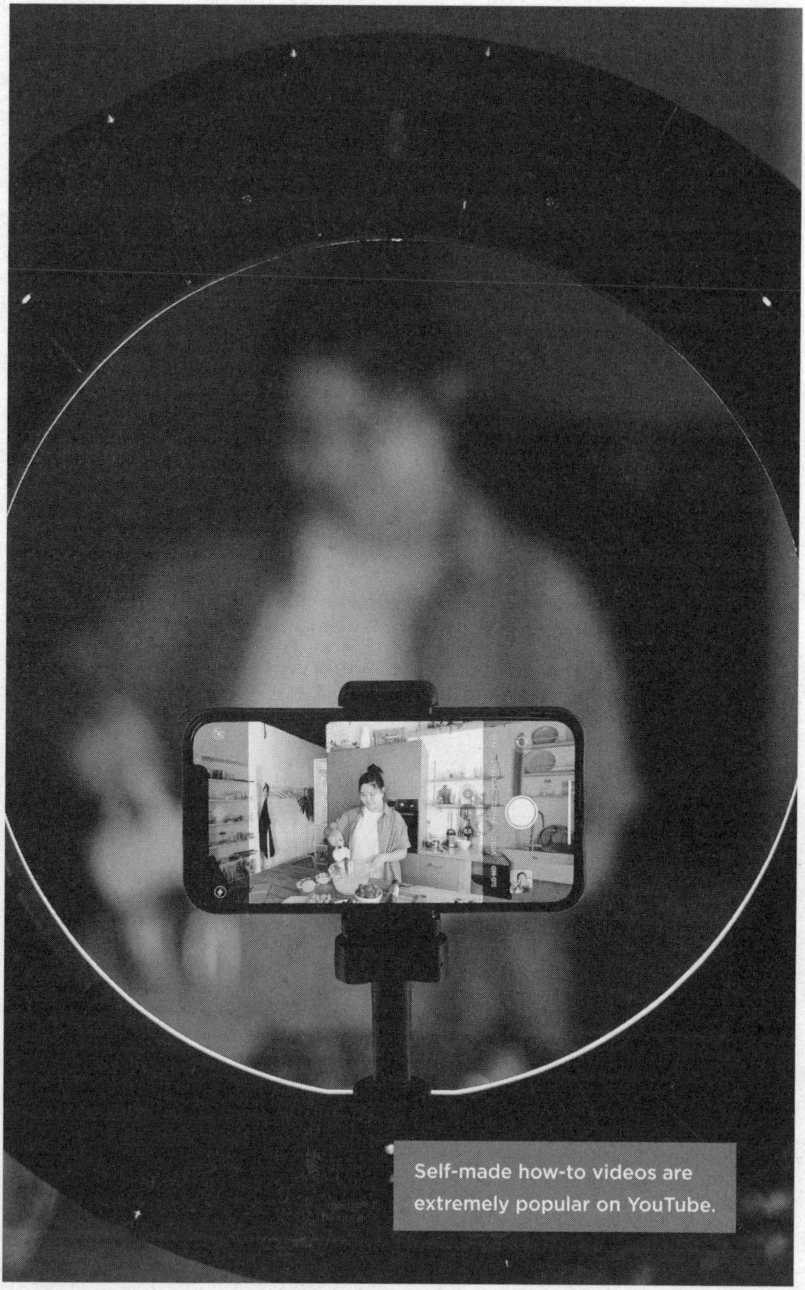

Self-made how-to videos are extremely popular on YouTube.

focused on search engines, Alphabet's interests stretched beyond that. Through a restructuring in 2015, Alphabet Inc. became the parent company, and now, it owns Google.

Leading Alphabet was Larry Page, with Sergey Brin as president, roles they kept until 2019, when both men stepped down from running their business on a daily basis. Sundar Pichai then took over as CEO of Google and Alphabet Inc., a role he continues to hold.

Each company within Alphabet Inc. focuses on a different subject. Under Calico, Alphabet is

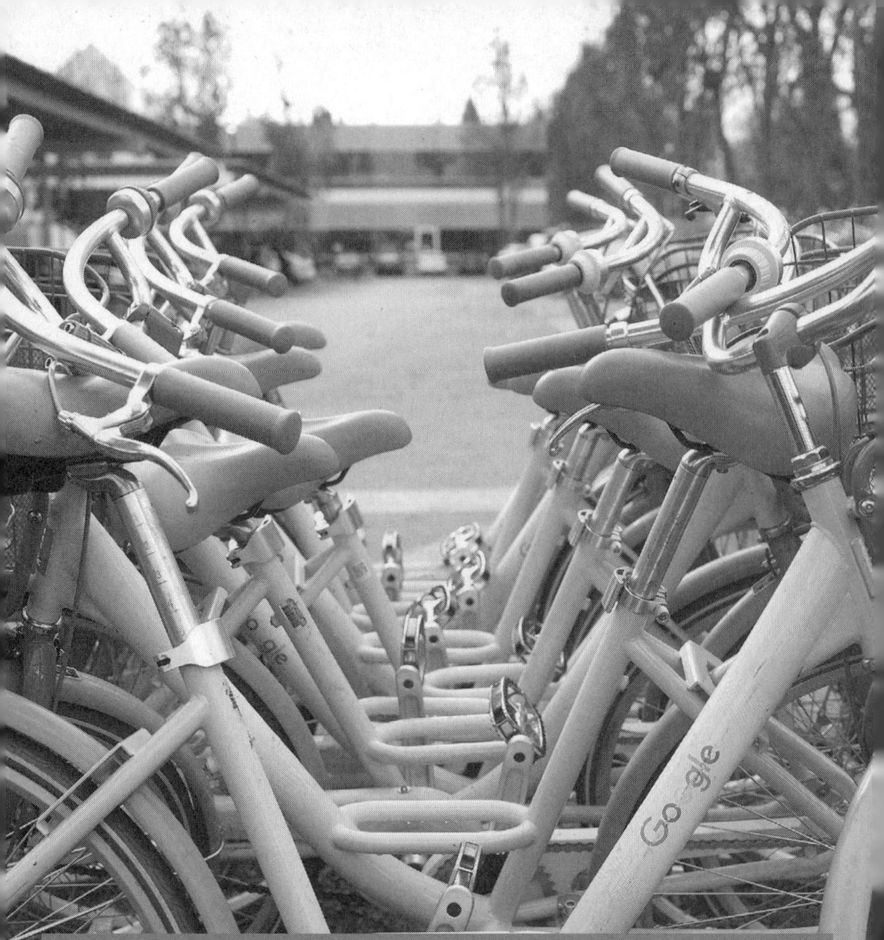

Founders and Friends

Company lore insists that Larry Page and Sergey Brin didn't like each other when they met as PhD students on the Stanford campus in 1995. They were known to challenge each other constantly and to argue often over silly ideas. But the two have been nearly inseparable since that time. Over the years, the two have maintained their friendship. After their new company, Alphabet Inc., was formed, Page and Brin stepped back from active involvement. Although no longer part of Google's daily world, Page and Brin remain active as cofounders, shareholders, and on the board of directors of Alphabet Inc.

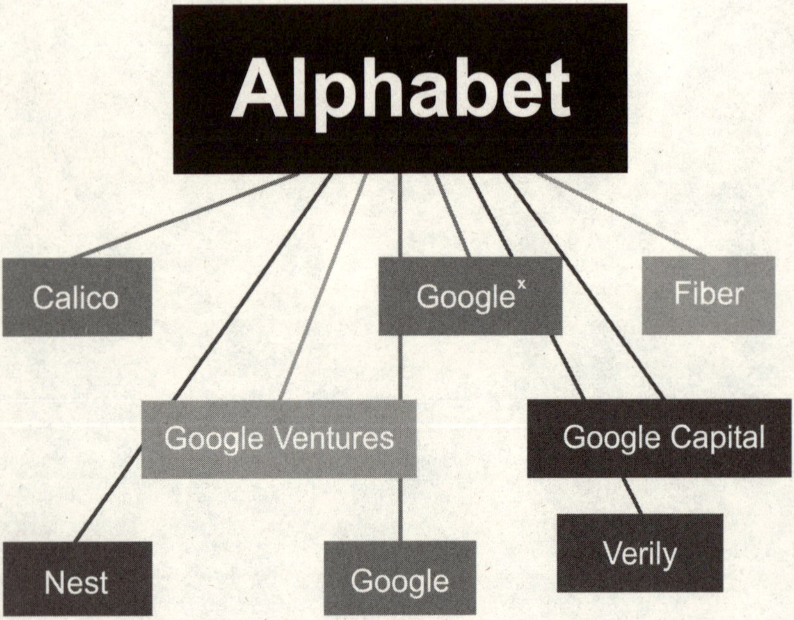
Alphabet
Calico
Google^x
Fiber
Google Ventures
Google Capital
Nest
Google
Verily

studying how to fight age-related diseases. Google X works on "big breakthroughs." Fiber strives to improve Internet speeds. Google Ventures helps fund other companies with their ideas. Google Capital invests in other technology firms, Nest focuses on smart home ideas, and Verily focuses on personal health.

Alphabet Inc. is also interested in studying longevity and the possibility of adding up to 100 years to the current human lifespan. "Illness and aging affect all our families," Page said. "With some . . . moonshot thinking around health care and biotechnology, I believe we can improve millions of lives."

"Moonshot thinking" is a literal goal of Alphabet's, too! With plans to someday travel to the moon, Google signed a 60-year lease for an airfield owned by the National Aeronautics

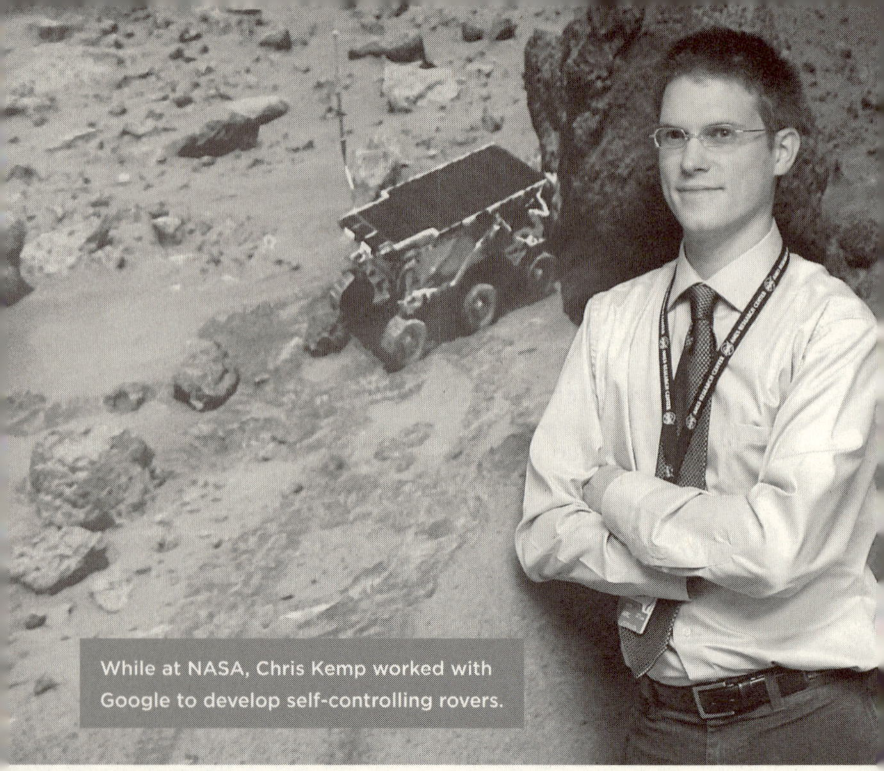

While at NASA, Chris Kemp worked with Google to develop self-controlling rovers.

and Space Administration (NASA), located next to Googleplex. In 2019, the two entities joined forces to work together on "**quantum supremacy**," the ability to compute in seconds what would have once taken thousands of years. Working with NASA is one more way Google is looking forward—and spaceward.

Another area of huge interest to Google is **Artificial Intelligence** (AI). AI uses computers in place of humans in many different scenarios. Google has long been interested in learning about AI and using AI as an effective way to organize information and make it accessible for people around the world. According to Jeff Dean, Google Chief Scientist, "We want to use AI to augment the abilities of people, to enable us to accomplish more and to allow us to spend more time on our creative endeavors."

In 2023, Google revealed plans to work AI into Google searches. It also wants to use AI within Gmail, adding a "Help Me Write" feature that will create instant replies to emails. AI features in "Magic Editor," a photograph editing tool, will be offered, as well.

AI is an area that can be extremely controversial, and Google is approaching its use cautiously. One problem with AI has been the creation of false or misleading information that sounds believable. Google is combating this problem by implementing safeguards to protect users from misinformation.

Despite its many successes, its abundant employee perks, and license to dream big, Google isn't perfect. Like many technology companies, Google was affected by a sluggish economy following the COVID-19 pandemic and in 2023 laid off thousands of employees. Worse, many of the employees were notified via email that they no longer had a job. It was a move in direct contrast to the company's previous "You belong here" and "Don't be evil" mottos.

Change is inevitable when dealing with a company as large and influential as Google. But the fact

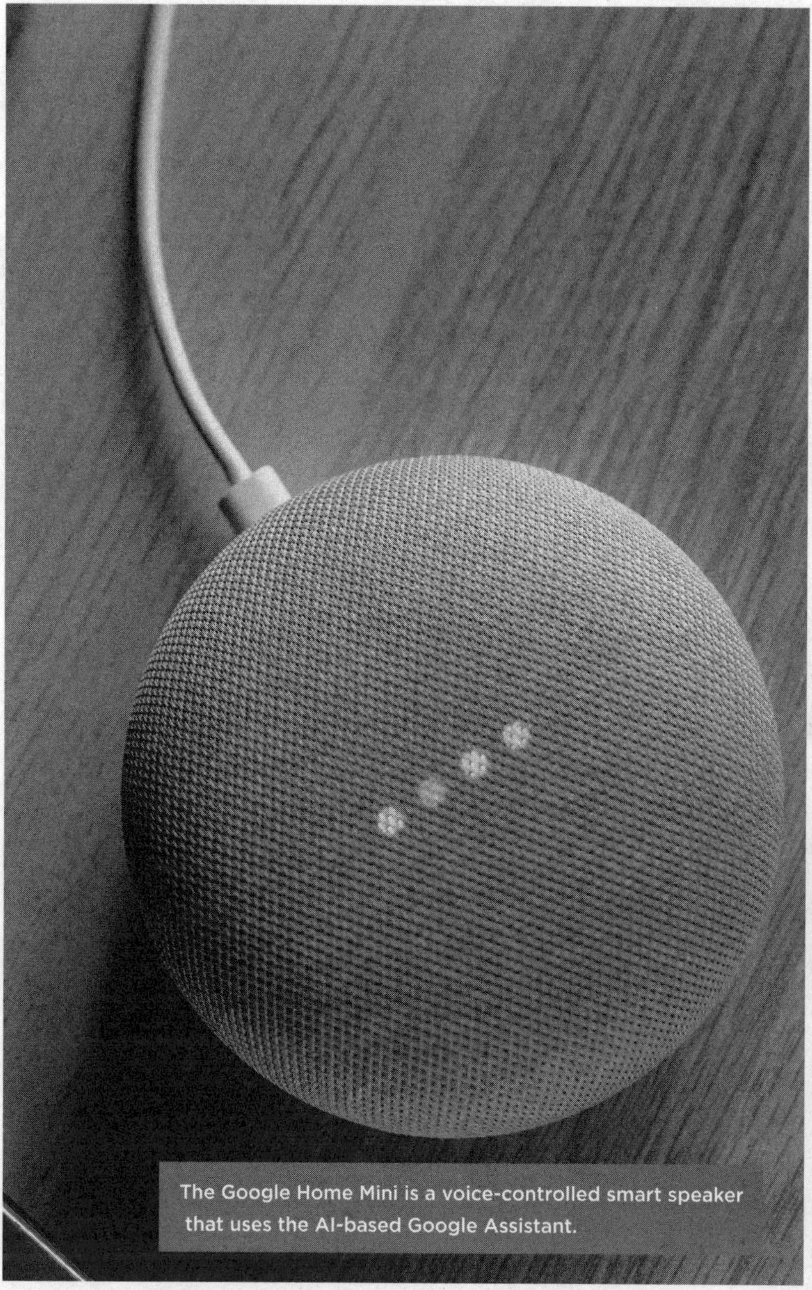

The Google Home Mini is a voice-controlled smart speaker that uses the AI-based Google Assistant.

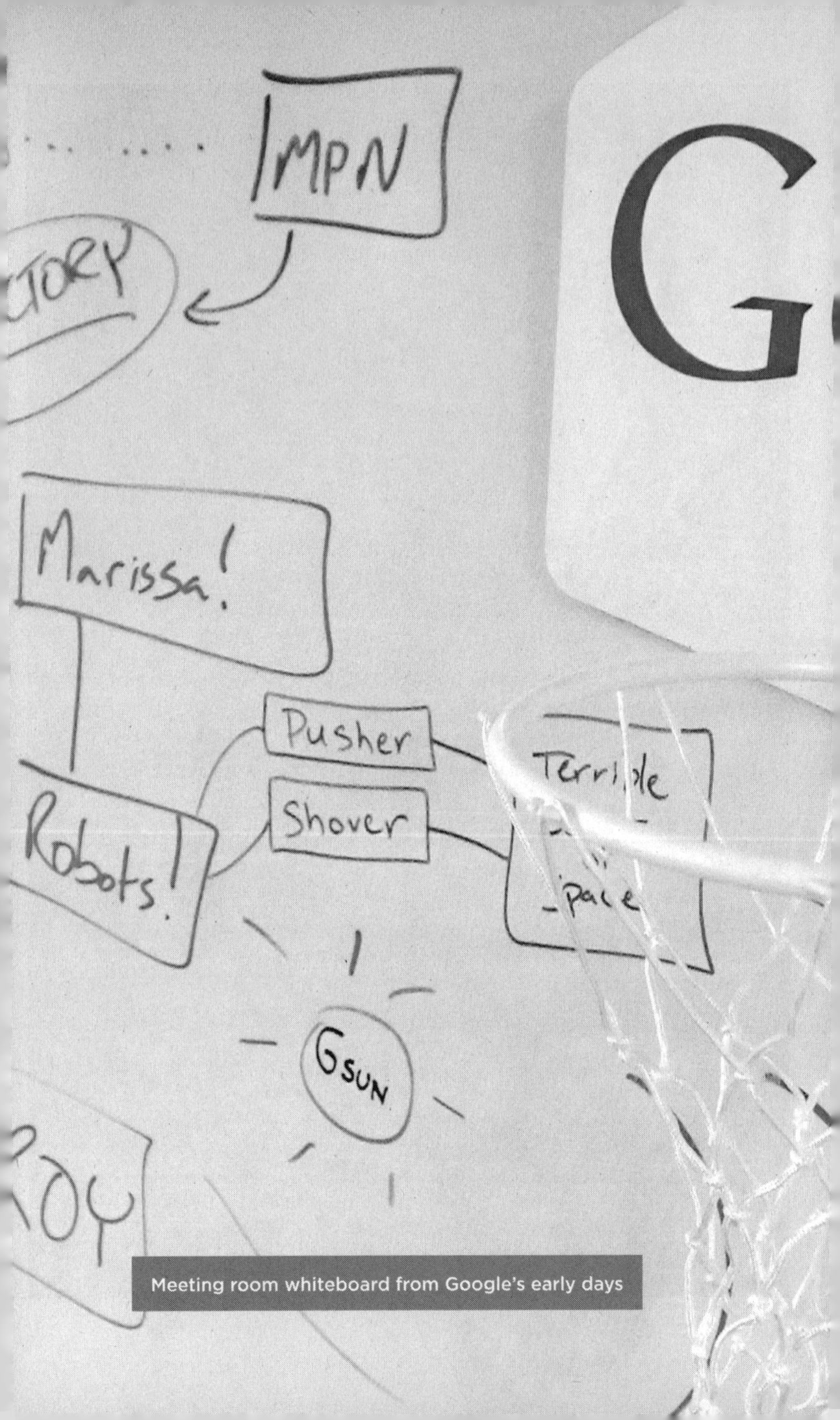

Meeting room whiteboard from Google's early days

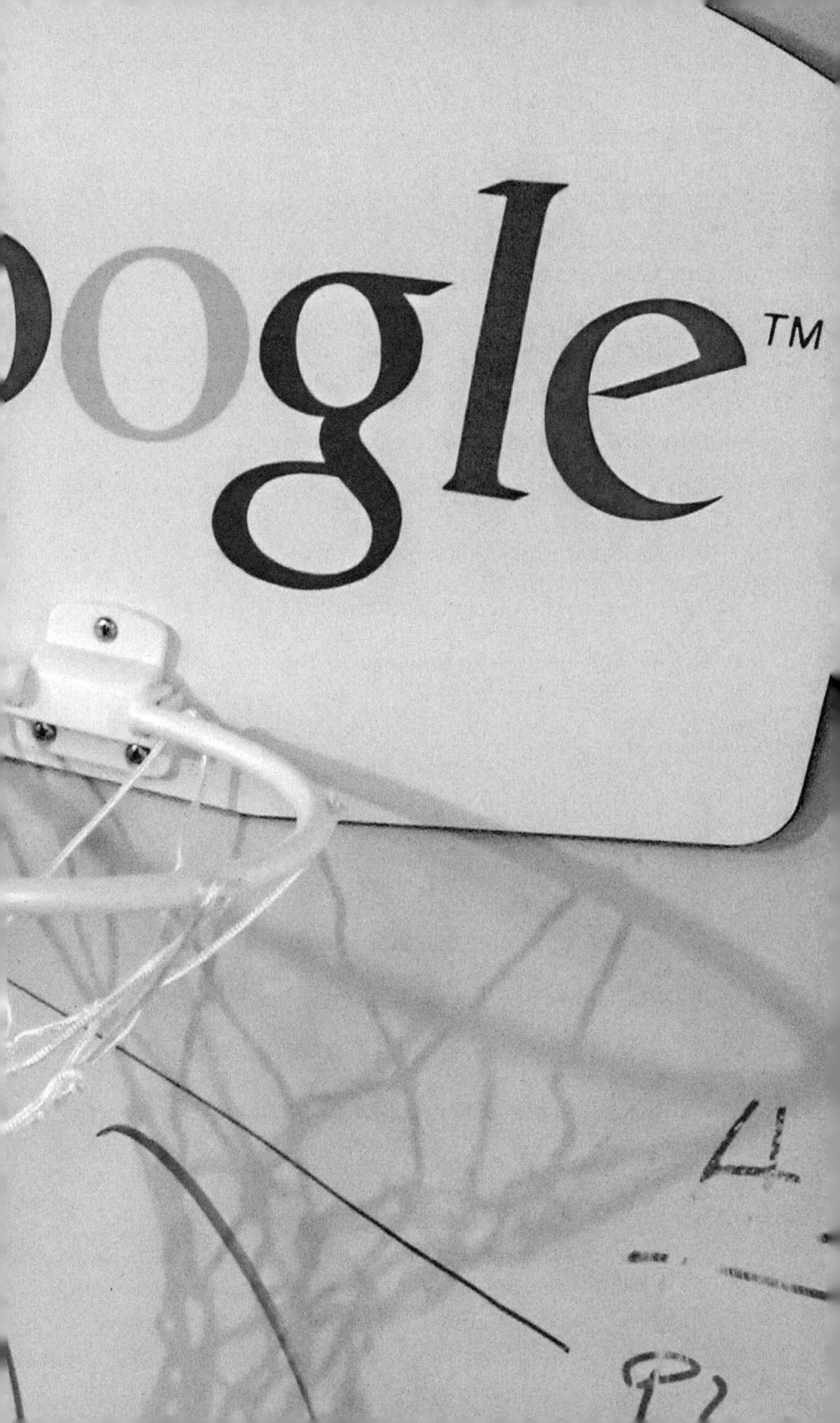
oogle™

that Google's many employees continue to actively seek new, creative ways to look at old problems says that Google is still a company to admire. Douglas Edwards, who worked for Google from 1999 to 2005, said, "After Google, I find myself impatient with the way the world works. Smart people, motivated to make things better, can do almost anything. I feel lucky to have seen firsthand just how true that is."

In 2015, after Alphabet Inc. was formed, Google's new motto became "Do the right thing." It appears to be a goal Google is continuing to aim for. What problems will Google try to solve next? One thing is certain—we're all sure to Google it.

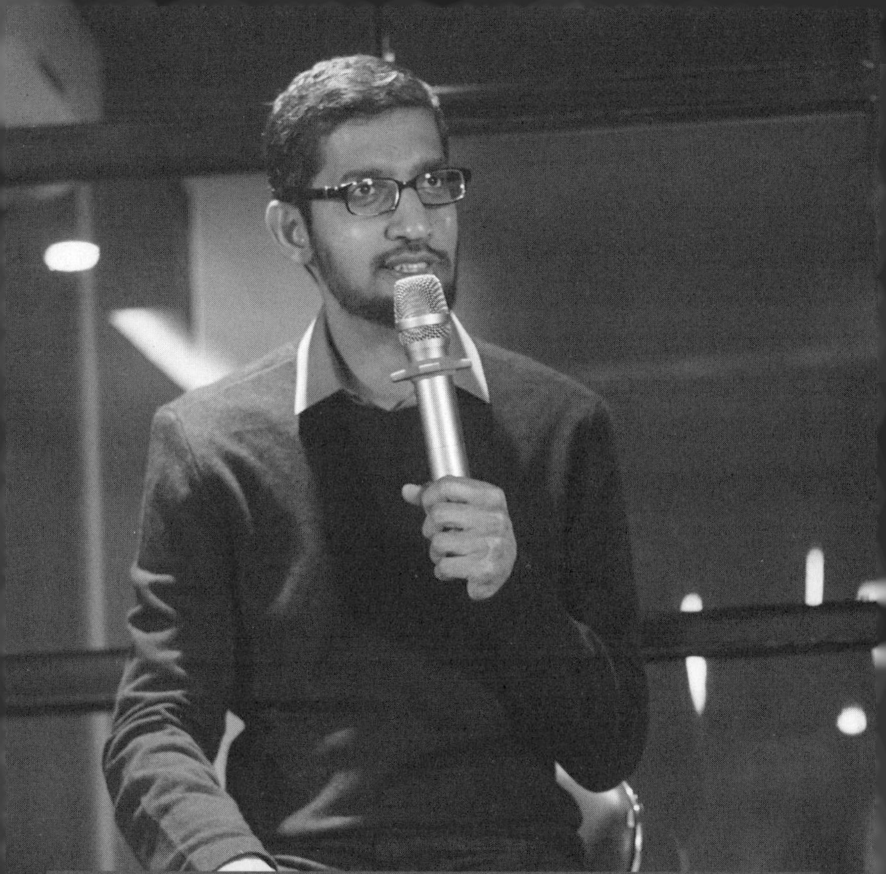

Meet the New Boss

Sundar Pichai joined Google in 2004 as part of product management and innovation. Pichai is largely credited with being the force behind Google Drive, a file storage and synchronization service. In 2015, Pichai became the new CEO of Google. That same year, he became CEO of Alphabet Inc., the company that was formed as Google's holding company. Pichai was born and educated in India, later earning advanced degrees from Stanford University and the Wharton School of Business. Pichai has led Google through interesting times, including the company's response to COVID-19 in 2020, when it sought to keep people informed and help people work and learn remotely.

Selected Bibliography

Edwards, Douglas. *I'm Feeling Lucky: The Confessions of Google Employee Number 59.* Boston: Houghton Mifflin Harcourt, 2011.

GMI Blogger. "YouTube Users Statistics 2023." Global Media Insight. August 17, 2023. https://www.globalmediainsight.com/blog/youtube-users-statistics.

Jackson, Rob. "100+ Google Apps That You Didn't Know Exist." Phandroid. April 10, 2018. https://phandroid.com/2018/04/10/google-apps-list-android.

Karch, Marziah. "What Is Google Play?" Lifewire. September 22, 2021. https://www.lifewire.com/what-is-google-play-1616720.

Schmidt, Eric, and Jonathan Rosenberg, with Alan Eagle. *Google: How Google Works.* New York: Grand Central Publishing, 2014.

Glossary

artificial intelligence
the ability of computer systems to perform tasks that normally require human intelligence, such as speech recognition and decision-making

board of directors
a committee that governs the actions of a business or organization

cross-platform computing software that is designed to be used on different types of computers or with different types of software

doctoral thesis a written paper based on research examining a new idea or point of view, especially as a requirement for an advanced academic degree

entity something with a distinct and independent existence

entrepreneur a person who organizes a new business venture and assumes the risks associated with it

executive a decision-making leader of a company, such as the president or chief executive officer (CEO)

gigabyte a unit of computer memory or data storage capacity equal to 1,024 megabytes, or 1 billion bytes

hard drive a computer part that reads and writes data, or information, on computer disks

hardware computers and the associated physical equipment directly involved in processing data

iconic widely known and easily recognized as representing something known for its excellence

incorporate to legally form into a company

initial public offering the process of offering shares in a company to the public for the first time

monopoly the exclusive control of the supply of a product or service

NASDAQ the National Association of Securities Dealers Automated Quotation system; a computerized system used to trade shares in public companies

profit the amount of money that a business keeps after subtracting expenses from revenues

quantum supremacy the experimental demonstration of a quantum computer's dominance and advantage over traditional computers by performing calculations at unmatched speeds

quarter one of four three-month intervals that together comprise the financial year

search engine a computer program that finds and retrieves files or data from a computer network or the Internet based on search terms entered by a user

stock option an opportunity for employees or investors in a company to buy or sell that company's stock; stock options are often given as part of an employee's benefits package

transitive verb a verb that requires an object to receive the verb

venture capital funds made available to small businesses that are starting out but show great potential for growth

Websites

28 Interesting Facts about Google
https://funfactsabout.net/interesting-facts-google
Discover bite-sized facts about the search-engine company.

Popular Google Doodle Games
https://sites.google.com/site/populardoodlegames/home
Play interactive games once featured on Google's home page.

The 10 Most Interesting Facts about Google
https://www.textmetrics.com/interesting-facts-google
Discover more fun facts about Google.

Index

More Titles from the Creative Companies Series

Jaico's creative companies series explores how today's great companies operate and inspires young readers to become the entrepreneurs and businessmen of tomorrow.

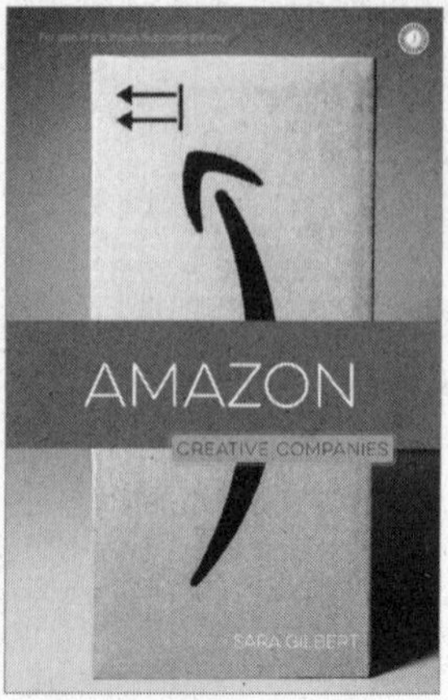

Amazon

Jeff Bezos founded Amazon in 1994 in a garage in Seattle, Washington, as an online bookstore. On July 16, 1995, Bezos launched the site, named after the vast Amazon River, and invited 300 friends to beta test it. Within 30 days, Amazon sold books across the U.S. and 45 countries, achieving meteoric success without press promotion. Today, Amazon is an e-commerce giant, offering a vast array of products and services while continuously innovating under Bezos's visionary leadership.

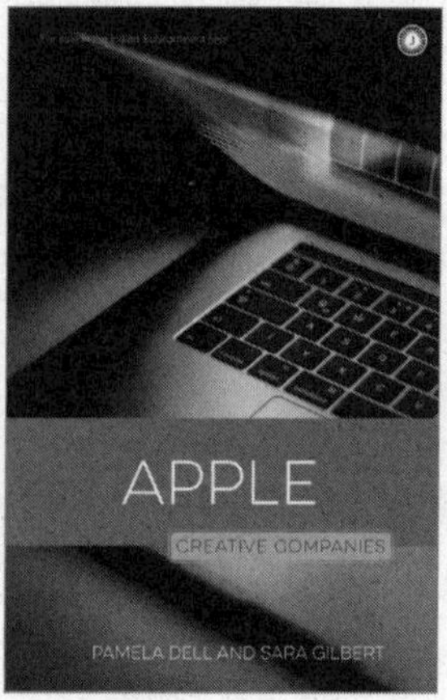

Apple

Did you know, Apple—the company behind your iPod, iPad, iPhone—began as a project shared by two ambitious boys in their computer club? When Steve Wozniak designed a computer in 1976, his friend Steve Jobs immediately saw its potential for a mass market. They found their first 'customer' at their local hobby club meeting and Apple Computer was born. Over the next 30-plus years, their company would transform the computer industry.

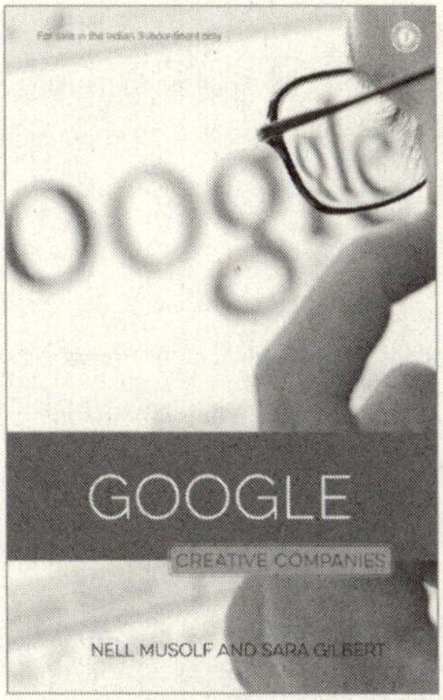

Google

This is the inspiring story of Larry Page and Sergey Brin, the founders of Google, who first met at Stanford University, in 1995. Most people would not even be aware of the fact that the very first Google office was in a friend's rented garage. Page and Brin soon began working on a likely doctoral thesis, which involved an attempt to download the complete World Wide Web, after which they would create a way to search the web, with the help of links. After many issues that involved budgeting and design, Google came into being.

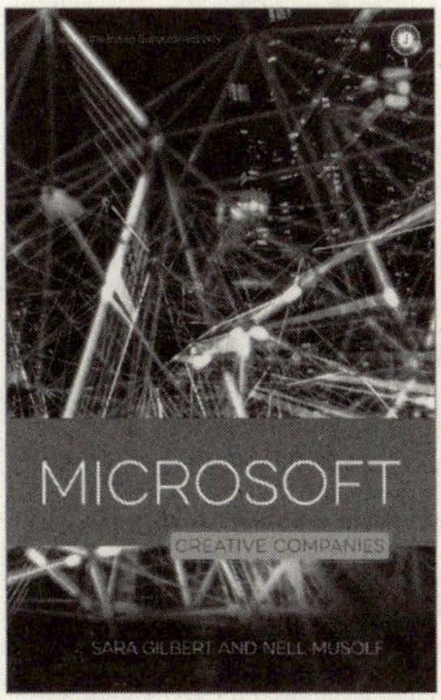

Microsoft

Bill Gates was in his second year of college at Harvard when he and his partner Paul Allen launched their own computer software company. Throughout their years at Lakeside School, Bill Gates and Paul Allen spent as much time as they could working on computers, becoming good friends in the process. Their company's impact has been such that the name 'Microsoft' has become virtually synonymous with computer software.

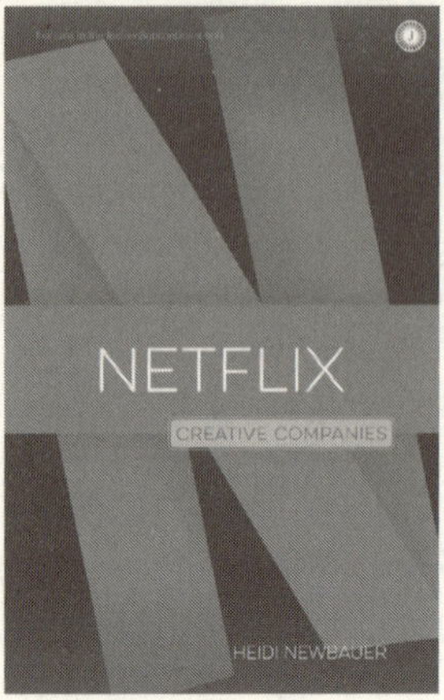

Netflix

Netflix was founded in 1997 by Reed Hastings and Marc Randolph in California as a DVD rental-by-mail service. Hastings was inspired after incurring a $40 late fee on a VHS rental, sparking the idea for a subscription-based model. In 2007, Netflix pivoted to online streaming, offering on-demand entertainment. By 2013, it expanded into original programming with hits like House of Cards. Today, Netflix is a global streaming powerhouse, revolutionizing how audiences consume movies and TV shows across the world.

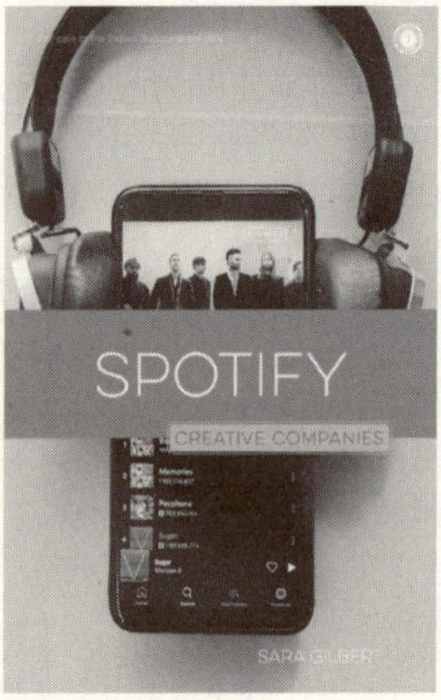

Spotify

Spotify was founded in 2006 by Daniel Ek and Martin Lorentzon in Stockholm, Sweden, as a response to music piracy. They envisioned a legal platform offering instant, affordable access to a vast music library. Launched in 2008, Spotify introduced a freemium model with ads and premium subscriptions. Its curated playlists and personalized recommendations reshaped music consumption. Today, Spotify is a global leader in audio streaming, boasting millions of tracks and podcasts, transforming how listeners discover and enjoy music worldwide..

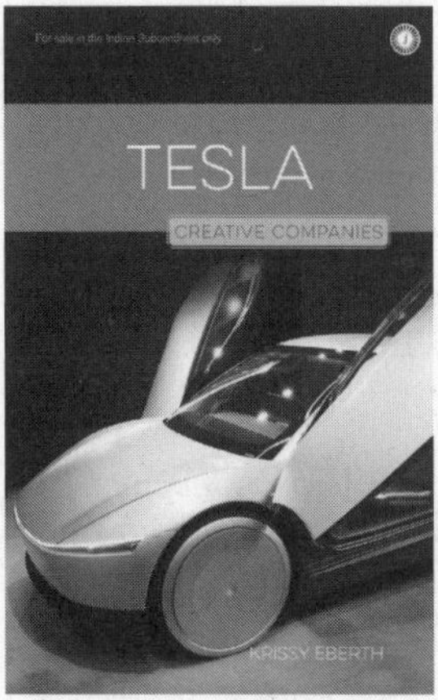

Tesla

Tesla was founded in 2003 by Martin Eberhard and Marc Tarpenning, with Elon Musk joining shortly after as an investor and chairman. Named after inventor Nikola Tesla, the company aimed to revolutionize transportation with electric vehicles. In 2008, Tesla launched the Roadster, proving EVs could be high-performance. Musk's leadership expanded Tesla's vision to sustainable energy solutions, including solar products and battery storage. Today, Tesla leads the EV industry, pushing innovation and advancements in autonomous driving.

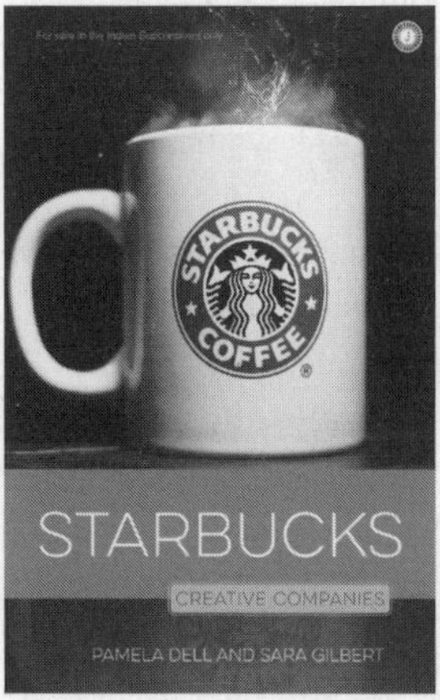

Starbucks

Starbucks was founded in 1971 by Jerry Baldwin, Zev Siegl, and Gordon Bowker in Seattle, Washington, as a single store selling high-quality coffee beans and equipment. Inspired by Italian coffee culture, Howard Schultz joined in 1982 and later transformed Starbucks into a café-centric brand, emphasizing premium coffee experiences. The first café opened in 1984, revolutionizing coffee consumption. Today, Starbucks operates thousands of locations globally.

JAICO PUBLISHING HOUSE

Elevate Your Life. Transform Your World.

ESTABLISHED IN 1946, Jaico Publishing House is home to world-transforming authors such as Robin Sharma, Sadhguru, Osho, the Dalai Lama, Deepak Chopra, Eknath Easwaran, Paramhansa Yogananda, Devdutt Pattanaik, Radhakrishnan Pillai, Morgan Housel, Napoleon Hill, John Maxwell, Brian Tracy, and Stephen Hawking.

Our late founder Mr. Jaman Shah first established Jaico as a book distribution company. Sensing that independence was around the corner, he aptly named his company Jaico ('Jai' means victory in Hindi). In order to service the significant demand for affordable books in a developing nation, Mr. Shah initiated Jaico's own publications. Jaico was India's first publisher of paperback books in the English language.

While self-help; religion and philosophy; mind, body and spirit; and business titles form the cornerstone of our non-fiction list, we publish an exciting range of current affairs, history, biography, art and architecture, travel, and popular science books as well. Our renewed focus on popular fiction is evident in our new titles by a host of fresh young talent from India and abroad.

Jaico's translations division publishes select bestselling titles in over 10 regional languages including Gujarati, Hindi, Kannada, Malayalam, Marathi, Tamil, and Telugu. These include titles from renowned national and international authors like Sudha Murthy, Gaur Gopal Das, Swami Mukundananda, Jay Shetty, Simon Sinek, Ankur Warikoo and Jeff Keller.

Visit our Website

Boasting one of India's largest book distribution networks, Jaico has its headquarters in Mumbai, with branches in Ahmedabad, Bangalore, Chennai, Delhi, Hyderabad, and Kolkata. This network ensures that our books reach all parts of the country, both urban and rural.